Philip St. George Cooke

The Conquest of New Mexico and California

An Historical and Personal Narrative

Philip St. George Cooke

The Conquest of New Mexico and California
An Historical and Personal Narrative

ISBN/EAN: 9783337208691

Printed in Europe, USA, Canada, Australia, Japan

Cover: Foto ©ninafisch / pixelio.de

More available books at **www.hansebooks.com**

THE CONQUEST

OF

NEW MEXICO AND CALIFORNIA;

AN HISTORICAL AND PERSONAL NARRATIVE.

By P. ST. GEO. COOKE,

BRIGADIER, BREVET MAJOR-GENERAL, U. S. A.

~~AUTHOR OF~~

'SCENES AND ADVENTURES IN THE ARMY; OR, ROMANCE OF MILITARY LIFE," ETC.

NEW YORK
G. P. PUTNAM'S SONS
182 FIFTH AVENUE
1878

CONTENTS.

I.
NEW MEXICO . . . . . . PAGE 1

II.
THE INSURRECTION IN NEW MEXICO AND THE FINAL CONQUEST 111

III.
THE INFANTRY MARCH TO THE PACIFIC . . 125

IV.
CALIFORNIA. 198

V.
FINAL CONQUEST OF CALIFORNIA . . . 263

PREFACE.

THE first historical narrative of the Conquests of New Mexico and California, is here offered to the public.

They were conquests as much of Nature's most inhospitable wastes, as of those primitive and isolated communities, and so exhibited great privations and labors; but some perilous ventures and exploits tinctured the whole with the old romance of the original Spanish invaders.

The conquerors were, for a year, almost beyond communication with government or countrymen, and these were wholly interested in the battles in Mexico; and thus it happened that a few soldiers and sailors, without sympathy or applause, achieved the only permanent fruits of the war.

This obscurity, and the remoteness of responsibility, led also to criminal intrigues as well as to patriotic sacrifices; and the time has come to give the world a connected and permanent record.

THE CONQUEST OF
NEW MEXICO AND CALIFORNIA.

I.

NEW MEXICO.

NOTWITHSTANDING the country by the policy and measures of the executive branch of the government had for many months been surely drifting toward war with Mexico, the public was electrified by the news of a collision of arms and brilliant victories at Palo Alto and Resaca de la Palma, May 8th and 9th, 1846. Thus was terminated,—" By the act of the Republic of Mexico," Congress declared on the 13th of May—our peace with all the world, which had continued so long that we had begun to look upon war as a chimera.

The first plans of the government were promptly developed : General Taylor crossed the Rio Grande and advanced with his army of " occupation " on the long line toward the city of Mexico; General Wool formed a column at San Antonio, Texas, for the invasion of Chihuahua; and Colonel Kearny, First Dragoons, organized a small force at Fort Leavenworth, Kansas, for the conquest of New Mexico, and ultimately of California. He marched June 30th.

Company F. Third Artillery sailed July 14th, from New York for California; and in September a regiment of New York Infantry Volunteers, Colonel Stevenson, also embarked for that destination; (They all arrived the following year).

Later a regiment of Missouri mounted volunteers, Colonel Price, was organized and marched early in the fall for Santa Fè.

Colonel Kearny had sent Captain James Allen, First Dragoons, to meet near Council Bluffs, Iowa, the migration westward of the Mormon community, which had shortly before been expelled from Nauvoo, Illinois; he was instructed to enroll a battalion of five hundred, to be organized under him as Lieutenant Colonel, at Fort Leavenworth; and to follow the army to Santa Fè. And, finally, Colonel Kearny had "demanded" two additional troops of first dragoons, on the Upper Mississippi, which had been ordered to the seat of war at the South, should follow and report to him. And accordingly on reaching St. Louis together, they encountered an order to that effect.

Their captains were E. V. Sumner and the writer; and they were inexpressibly disappointed. New Mexico was then supposed to be the only objective of this column.

We embarked for Fort Leavenworth, and marched from there July 6th.

I find the following in my diary for July 21st. "The howls of wolves, in which I ever took a singular pleasure, swelling upon the night breeze, set my pen in motion. This has been a jolly day for Mark Tapleys—a very hot and still day with swarms of horse flies. I came ahead to hunt, (a solitary heron was all I saw larger than a fly,) and I was forced to stop, dismount and brush my horse vigorously for a half hour, until the column came up to make the fight more equal. Then a slight air from behind brought with us a cloud of dust. We turned off, near a mile, over rough ground it happened, to 'noon' at the bank of the Arkansas (it is a horrid practice). After that a storm threatened, and the wind shifted right ahead, which for dust was nearly as bad; and finally it came with a great blast from the North, which fairly blew us, for a moment, out of the road!

"Now the thunders are rolling and promise a wet night, to which we are well nigh hardened. A week ago we had very severe hail, which stampeded the horses, and one was lost. Writing back, I may mention that one day we passed through vast multitudes of buffaloes; the next day there were many, and since very few. A horse and some mules, allowed to run loose on the march, effectually knocked up, we thought, took, very late in life, a fancy for freedom, and ran off with a herd of buffalo; they were with difficulty recovered after a chase of six miles!"

July 28*th.*—Rain or shine, we have averaged 28 miles! Another dull week, but why not mention that our prairie and muddy river monotony was relieved by not unpleasant reminiscences to me, as we passed at 100° W. Lon. near, but on the south side, that rare feature, a small grove to which the writer three years ago, had, of right, given a name—

Jackson's Grove, for there in emulation of that great soldier's *decision* he had crossed a force through the flooded Arkansas into doubtful territory of unsurveyed boundaries, to attack and disarm two hundred men, the "Army of Texas," who lay in wait to capture large Mexican caravans, as soon as they should pass the river above, from under his escort. Citizens of a territory on which he now marched with military impartiality, to make war in their turn!

And forty or fifty miles on, we passed by "Chouteau's Island" where, when quite a youth, he made first acquaintance with those savage Scythians, the Comanches, and had the fortune, detached with thirty veteran infantry, to face and break the charge of full five hundred, while a six-pounder sent round shot above his head.

July 31*st*.—Most pleasant it was to-day to come in sight of the white tents of the army, spread out in the green meadows of the river; a multitude of animals grazing; the life and stir of preparation; mounted orderlies in motion; old friends flocking out with smiles of welcome."

August 1*st*.—' The army of the West' consists of a regiment of cavalry, two batteries of horse artillery, two companies of infantry—all raw volunteers,—and six troops of First Dragoons, U. S. A.; about seventeen hundred rank and file.

The march is ordered for to-morrow. Our camp is about nine miles below " Bent's Fort," a trading post which has become more familiar by name than any national forts; and is in reality the only *fort* at the West.

About noon I was sent for, and the general greatly surprised me by a proposition that I should set out in advance, with a flag of truce to Santa Fè, some three hundred miles.

In our conversation, he assured me that he attached much importance to it—that he had *waited* for me; and otherwise would have sent his chief of staff; that if there should be fighting, I would undoubtedly return and meet him before it began.

I go to-morrow, with twelve picked men of my troop. Mr. James Magoffin of Kentucky and Señor Gonzales of Chihuahua have permission to accompany me—both merchants of caravans, which rather singularly, are now journeying to New Mexico, and beyond.

August 2d.—I set out at the same hour the army marched, and fell in with the general at its head; and so rode with him to Bent's Fort. My mission was not soothing to the regret at being turned aside from the stirring war scenes at the south; it was in fact a pacific one. The general had just issued a proclamation of annexation of all the territory *east of the Rio Grande*; the government thus adopting the old claim of Texas; and thus, manifestly, in a statesman's view, a bloodless process would lead to its confirmation in the treaty of peace; and the population would be saved from the bitterness of passing *sub jugum.* The difficulty of a half measure remains; it cuts the isolated province in two! there must be an influential Micawber in the Cabinet.

At a plaintive compliment, that I went to plant the olive, which he would reap a laurel, the general endeavored to gloss the barren field of toil, to which his subordinates at least, were devoted; and rather unsuccessful, he then revealed his ulterior instructions for the conquest of California. He had been promised the grade of brigadier general, to date with the march for that territory. A regiment or two would follow us to New Mexico.

New deserts to conquer! That was giving to our monotonous toils a grandeur of scale that tinctured them with adventure and excitement.

At the Fort I stopped to procure a pack mule. I found it excessively crowded; a focus of business and curiosity: it is the land of Scythian Comanches, the audacious Cheyennes, here were many races and colors,—a confusion of tongues, of rank and condition, and of cross purposes. Meanwhile the long column of horse continually passed, fording the river; but officers were collecting stragglers, and straggling themselves.

My business completed, I found Don Santiago, as the Mexicans call Mr. Magoffin, had been promised a stirrup cup, if any private nook was found possible. A long hot desert ride was in prospect; and Mr. Bent had an ice house; our patience was strengthened. At last vigilant eyes recognized a signal from a flat house top. With unconscious mien, we wound our way through the thirsty and curious crowd, up a winding stair, and, dexterously we thought, into a sentry box of a room, and lo! a long necked straggler—*genus* Pike—slipped in with us! We gave him a chilling stare; he took it comfortably. A pitcher covered with a dew of promise, caught our eyes; it brimmed with broken ice, and there was a suggestive aroma which softened our hearts. We fraternized, and soon finished the glorious punch.

At last we were ready; but my new pack mule instantly dashed in full and clattering charge through scattering stragglers; away flew cups and pans,— and away started skittish nags with vociferous riders. Juan and Jose charged after, through the loud laughing crowd; I laughed, myself, despite my luckless mess kit. The foolish mule, so resentful of an unwonted crupper, soon succumbed to the more familiar virtues of Juan's lazo; order was restored, and we followed the long procession fording the Arkansas River.

All attempt to pass this wonderfully mobile army was found to be vain; and so, with my handful of troopers I was content to follow, for many hours; amused at times by the humors of my companions, Magoffin and Gonzales, who drove somewhat in advance. As we passed in the vicinity of several corrals and camps of the caravan merchants—who were required to await the motions of the army—I could see Juan gallop off, bottle in hand; for his master, whose provision of wine defied all human exigencies, had failed in the rare article of brandy, which he also appreciated. "Won't they say," he cried out, "what a clever fellow that is in the black carretilla to send us down a bottle of brandy;" but Juan returned light handed from each visit.

Señor M. now and then gave his fine horses a short gallop; then Gonzales would with violent efforts, force his shabby mules to keep close up,— only to be checked, very suddenly, to a walk. No American would have risked such looking mules for a day's journey; but the Mexicans, not learned nor wise, are masters in the science of mules! Although in this case there was no secret, there *is* a mystery about it; Jose, while G. drove, rode by the side of the team, almost incessantly and laboriously whipping!

A hot dusty ride we had through the flat wilderness; the army made that day, a march of thirty-seven miles. That fact was enough to indicate that it had an extraordinary leader, and that it might successfully defy all rule and precedent.

At last, as the sun was setting, I saw the troops leaving the road to camp; and although there was no indication of water beyond, I kept on; and after I had entirely passed, came in sight of some tents, and directed there my course; I found it the camp of the small battalion of infantry, who had marched the previous day.

We were hospitably welcomed; but there was scant grass for the few animals, and the water of the little stream, the Timpe, was a weak but decided solution of Epsom salts. Variety in diet is pleasing; but extremes not always. Capt. Angney, the commander, had procured at the fort, some molasses,—for the consideration of a dollar the pint—and that, with strong thirst, helped down the tepid Timpe. After all its effects were moderate.

Next morning we were off betimes with the infantry; the scenery all day was wild, and strange to us; bare of trees or grass,—save on the ridges where cedars and pines were to be seen; our information indicated no water short of a very long march.

But by taking a horse trail, and passing along a ridge, near noon, a good spring was found, and there we passed several hours under the shade of piñon trees, indulging in lunch, with claret wine and piñon nuts for dessert.

In the afternoon, the road being very difficult, I got far ahead of the carriages; near sundown I overtook numerous infantry stragglers, suffering from extreme thirst. Just at dark, I saw the battalion camp fires, but beyond a rocky and deep ravine which we could not cross. We managed, however, to get water, and bivouacked above under the little cedar trees. I heard my sergeant discussing with his party, that extraordinary infantry, which, with our fine horses, we could not pass; but he said, "if regulars were to straggle so, they would be considered as *mutinizing*.

August 4th.—We pushed on, over more bad ground, twenty miles to the next water, a mere muddy pond, where we found antelope and elk. After a short nooning, we saw the battalion coming, and Don Santiago expressing great apprehension of being "run over by that long legged infantry," we hastened to depart. We stopped late, on the Las Animas, also called the Purgatory, at the foot of the Raton Mountain. It is a fine, bold stream, which mouths fifteen miles below Bent's Fort. It has a well known cañon; its high precipices protect groves and grass; and, besides the warm shelter for animals, there is said to be good grazing the year round.

Next morning we followed the difficult road up the Raton; this mountain is seventy-five hundred feet high, and is well covered with lofty pines, oaks, etc.; it has been dreaded for the baggage train.

⟨ There is a shorter route to Santa Fè which passes no mountain, or very bad road; but this one by Bent's Fort was selected as better meeting the needs of the expedition. The other, the "Cimarone Route," is much more deficient in fuel, and has a dreaded *jornada ;* while that by Bent's Fort has in the fort on the frontier a *quasi* base.

I followed a small stream nearly to the top of the mountain, the carriages far behind. There I stopped for nooning, on an inviting green slope, very near the streamlet, and in the shadow of some grand old pines.

Fatigued as I was, there was much that was delightful in this solitary repose, besides the fresh mountain air. Lowlanders never see such pure blue skies; and now snow-white clouds drifting over, intensified the blue above, and by their shadowings, added life and beauty to the landscape pictures below; and there was a gentle breeze, just enough to give that spirit-like music of the pine leaves, and in harmony with the purl of the mountain brook.

Here were varying and very perfect sensuous enjoyments, which were elevating too; their effects on me were so joyous and abstracting, that two fawns came down the opposite slope and drank ten paces off, without arousing the destructive hunter's instinct, or at all reminding me of the rifle at my side.

At last, with sounds of wheels and whips, came the carriages;. Magoffin humorous with affected anger at the hard chase I had led him.

He was in the vein to-day; reclining on the grass, after lunch, he made a long speech to Gonzales, in the most sonorous Spanish, about liberty and equality, and the thousand advantages of being conquered by our arms. Then, chuckling, he swore the old rascal would get himself in the calaboose as soon as he got to Chihuahua. He then held up, and addressed a pocket cork-screw, which, he said he had carried eight years. "You have cost me a thousand—five thousand dollars; but what do I care for except a bottle of wine every day; I work this way on purpose to keep you; what is money good for? I would not say to a bottle of champagne, 'I won't, I cannot use you,' for a million of dollars. I travel this way every year over deserts just to be able to have my wine and educate my children. I will educate them as long as they can stand it; give them all sorts of teachers, to teach them all they can pound into them; and when they say 'we have beaten into their heads all that we *possibly* can,' then I will be satisfied; that is all I want to do for them." But no idea can be given of the embellishment which his droll manner adds to his eccentric humor.

The view from the top of the mountain is very extensive—very fine; it embraces not only the Spanish Peaks, but Pike's Peak, above one hundred miles to their north.

The descent was long and rough; and my foolish mule made another scamper, scattering my humble but very important mess kit. The carretillas did not come up, and I slept without shelter on the flat and barren bank of an upper stream of "Red River"—the Canadian of the maps. Next day it was the same, and I bivouacked at a water pool. The third day they overtook me, at noon, at the Riado. Don Santiago's claret was very welcome again; he had broken his carriage pole, descending the mountain, but declared it was now much stronger than before.

In the afternoon we separated again, passing strange wild scenery. We suffered want of water—passing at sunset a wide shallow pond saturated with some vile salts. The road ascended then, to what seemed a great inclined shelf of the mountain.

We rode very late, hoping for water. The light of even a full moon gave an imperfect idea of the strange scenery, but seemed to excite vague imaginings. On the soft road we did not disturb the profound and lifeless silence. Imagine then our wonder, to hear unwarned, several rapid explosions, identical in sound to near cannon shots. Only then we saw coming over the near horizon of a mountain ridge, the rapid invasion of our serene sky by a thunder cloud in black points which were not unlike the column heads of an attacking army. And then we were in a shower, with moonlight all around;

and very soon passed on this phantom cloud, leaving all serene as if it had not been.

But it is very vain to attempt to describe it all —to excite sympathetic appreciation; it is the mere chance of a wanderer's lifetime to witness such a spectacle, with all its attendant and weird surroundings.

I observed for some time a singular dark streak to our left; and at last, partly in curiosity, discovered it to be a chasm, a precipitous ravine, with a little stream of water; and so there we spent the rest of the night.

Next day, August 8th, we passed along the very singular valley, where Fort Union was afterward built, and a ride of twenty-eight miles brought us to the Mora, a bright stream which here breaks out of the high table land, a kind of base to the high Rocky Mountain ridge which had long been on our right. Here we first saw houses, two or three, and cattle and sheep. This settlement was not an outgrowth of the Territory, but an approach of civilization; the proprietors being an Englishman and an American; a very doubtful civilization, too, adulterated by wilderness habits and Indian intercourse.

Next day sixteen miles over a prairie table-land brought us to its steep road-limit, from whence we overlooked a valley with a stream; we saw corn-fields and herds; but where was Los Vegas, which should be there? I saw, I thought, a great clay bank, a singular one indeed, but I thought it must be an extensive brick-yard and kilns. In fact it was Vegas; the dwellings being in low square blocks, sides and tops of sun-dried yellow bricks or adobes; the streets, and a large square, being of the same color.

Then we saw the people running and riding about in excitement and apparent confusion; mounting in hot haste, driving in herds of ponies, cattle, goats. I hardly believed the appearance, on the bluff, of my party of horse to be the occasion of it all; and as I drew nearer I doubted more and more, for a large party came galloping in my direction.

This hostile demonstration was too doubtful, in my view, for momentary solution; if it occurred to me to display a flag of truce, I was unprepared to do so, and could only continue my advance in the best order to meet the worst. All doubt was soon solved by these eccentric cavaliers, formidable at least in appearance, passing at the gallop to our left. I marched on with increasing astonishment, tinged with a shade of mortification. I soon learned that this very characteristic introduction to New Mexican life, was caused by the wild Indians having killed a shepherd or two, at a distance of two leagues, and driven off their flock. And such was the measure of New Mexican efficiency—to gallop off in confusion, and without provision, to a pursuit, in which, if the robbers were overtaken, it would be at the moment when their own horses were quite blown, or exhausted.

I rode with Mr. M. to the home of the alcalde, who was his old acquaintance: quite a number of his neighbors visited us and expressed pleasure at their prospects, and some whiskey was handed round in an earthen cup.

There is some mixture of stone in the structure of the houses; that material being here very convenient and suitable; but the village, with its small fields, scarcely fenced, differed little from those of our Pawnees in appearance; these dwellings are smaller and square instead of round; fine mountain streams are near, and are conducted—as usual—by the main canal of irrigation, through the place.

While my horses were fed, we sat down to a dinner; it was composed of a plate, for each, of poached eggs, and wheaten tortillas; seeing some cheese on a small pine table, I asked for a knife to cut it;—the old man went to a hair trunk, and produced a very common pocket knife. The room had a smooth earthen floor; it was partly covered by a kind of carpeting of primitive manufacture, in white and black—or natural coloring of the wool;—it is called Jerga; around the room, mattresses, doubled pillows, and coverlids, composed a kind of divan; the walls were whitewashed, with gypsum,—which rubbing off easily, a breadth of calico was attached to the walls above the divan; there was a doll-like image of the virgin, and two very rude paintings on boards and some small mirrors; the low room was ceiled with puncheons, supporting earth;—there were several rough board chairs. The alcalde's dress was a calico shirt,—very loose white cotton drawers or trowsers, and over them another pair— also very loose,—of leather, open far up at the outer seams. There appeared to be servants,—wild Indians of full blood. This may serve for a general picture.

The alcalde—profanely surnamed *Dios*—gave me a very singular missive to his inferior magistrate of the next village; it required him to furnish ten men to watch my camp, that the Utahs should not steal my horses, and my men might sleep. He sent as I afterward learned, a swift express by the mountain paths, to the Governor at Santa Fè.

We passed, a few miles beyond Vegas, the best named natural " gate " I had ever seen,—through a ridge some four hundred feet high. The scenery of my Piedmont route—from Raton to Santa Fè— now greatly improved; wooded hills, many bright streams, some natural parks. There had been a shower here, and the red gravel road, and the buffalo grass, under stately pines and cedars, looked fresh swept and washed; the air was exhilarating, but the charm over all was the almost dazzling sky.

Nine miles brought us to a commanding hill-top, with a view of an extensive valley,—open, smooth, cultivated;—a bold stream was in its meadows; there were herds and flocks on the slopes, and groves of pines; the mountains surrounded all.

Tecolote,—very like Las Vegas—was in the bottom of the valley; the scene must have been peaceful; for apparently forgetful of the war, I left my escort unsaddling for the night, and without showing a flag, rode a quarter of a mile to the large crowd gathered at the entrance of the village; saluting them, I inquired for the alcalde, and in barbarous Spanish, told him as I presented the note, that I wanted not men, but corn. And I got some, at three dollars a bushel; and a sheep for a dollar and a half; and milk and eggs and chickens were offered for sale at my little camp.

With Don Santiago and Señor G. came some of their acquaintances to supper in my tent; one of the latter contributed a pocket-flask of aguadiente, which could be recommended as strong. Gonzales gave *it* cordial reception; and to his friends,—at second hand,—the liberty and annexation lectures of the *Don* with additions and embellishments.

August 10th.—The first novelty I saw this morning was a flock of milk goats going to pasture for the day, in charge of a boy and two shepherd dogs. Singular it is, that the Spaniards occupied on this continent, and expanded over, precisely all the region,—

of mountain and high arid plains,—so resembling Spain, that their national customs of agriculture by irrigation, transportation by pack mules and asses, the raising of flocks, etc., were strictly preserved; and so natural and necessary was their introduction, that it may account in part for their present homogeneousness with the aborigines.

I was struck on the road, with the number of people passing, and their lively mood. We fell in with one very merry party; chiefly the family of an old man, as lively and active as a monkey, and not much larger; perhaps it was a wedding party;—a very pretty girl rode on an ass, which took into its solemn head to penetrate our procession of large horses; and in spite of her guiding stick, she was in danger; then a young man who rode a mule, came spurring to her rescue, and seizing the donkey with great vehemence by each ear, dragged him forth; the girl's face was very expressive both of humor and anxiety; as for the old man, his excitement carried his donkey to a gallop, while the hills rang with his shouts and laughter.

San Miguel, built of dull red adobes, in a dull red surrounding country, was now before us on the first hill beyond the Pecos; this stream is here very pleasant to the eye, running swift and clear, a foot or two deep and a hundred wide, through meadows green with wheat and corn,—this last only three feet up to the tassel,—the former, spring wheat, reaped in September. The town turned out to see us, but I made no stay. The road turning up the Pecos valley, passed for some twenty miles along the rather broken declivity,—hills and deep clay gullies,—of, what to all appearance, was a respectable mountain six hundred feet high; but which in fact is the break of a famous vast table land, destitute of water.

We got on about fifteen miles; caught now and then by a mountain shower, of this the rainy season; and camped at a rain pool, under some fine trees.

August 11th.—The Don last night bragged very much of his cook, and of his manufacture of soup of a turtle he had captured. It was poison to me; and so I had to supplement it with a small lump of opium, which, with little relief to my agony, prostrated my strength. And so I had to ride all day in his carriage, and got only a passing view of some interesting ruins; [to Americans, especially, who, with a reputation for boasting, are worst off,—of all things

—for antiquities; and so it happens we make much of "broken pottery;" and when we find in the woods any eccentric hillocks or mounds, or the ruins of adobe huts, straightway a cipher is added to their probable age, and they are pressed into the service of American archæology]. It was the ruins of a walled town called Pecos—which I have visited since—standing on a hill-top, between two branches of Pecos River; three mountain ridges and three valleys meet, (it is something like Harper's Ferry,) with vistas here of far off peaks. A beautiful panorama! On the bare mountain sides of neutral tints, in this pure rare atmosphere the sun plays master painter,—with floating clouds for his help—and ever changes the picture as he moves.

Here we see, only partially ruined, the temples of two religions which met in rivalry—the Aztec, with unceasing altar fire, and that of Rome, with its graven images; the former an ignorant, honest superstition with a basis of morality; the latter, degenerated in this far isolation, steeped in immorality, embodied in spectacles and ceremonies, and degrading all that is high and holy to the level of sense—the depths of superstition.

Some contend that the Roman Catholic religion was only grafted on the Aztec; that the two were harmoniously blended; this is surely affirmed of the present religion of the Pueblos here. It is stated, (but it sounds like a tradition, such is the ignorance of this people, without a press,) that only some seven years ago, the sacred fire was taken from the estufa here, by a small remnant of the tribe, to the Pueblos of Zuñi, not very distant to the south-west.

But we drove on, and some miles brought us to the wild rocky cañon, where, a few days later, four or five thousand men were very strongly posted to give battle to our army. I took care to find out, however, and observed *how*, it could be turned. My escort got ahead; and when, six or eight miles from Santa Fè, I determined to stop, they, not having discovered the water, had gone on; and so in much suffering and uneasiness I lay down under a bush; my stomach refusing every thing, until after midnight, when I drank a little claret wine, which Don Santiago had kindly insisted on putting within my reach.

Next morning, August 12th, we pushed on, and on the high barren hills, almost in sight of Santa Fè, to my great relief, the escort joined me: I mounted then, and we approached the "city." At the foot, or at the extremity of a main ridge of the Rocky Mountains, in the midst of a grey barren country without grass, and in the sandy flat valley of a mountain stream, there it was, like a very extensive brick-yard indeed.

Fording the bright and rocky little river, I rode through a long crooked street, passing crowds of people who generally returned my salutation of *buenos dias*, "good morning to you." I lost sight of the carretillas, and going rather at random, suddenly found myself in front of the quarter of a large guard, who at view of my horsemen, howled out their "alarm," with so hideous intonation, that I mistook it for a menace. For the first time, I thought it would not be amiss to air my flag of truce; so I placed a white handkerchief on the point of my sabre, and the officer of the guard advancing to meet me, I announced my mission in a sentence of very formal book-Spanish; he gave me a direction, to the right I thought, and looking up a narrow street, I saw a friendly signal, pushed on, and emerging, found myself and party on the plaza, crowded by some thousands of soldiers and countrymen, called out en masse, to meet our army. We made our way with some difficulty, toward the "palace," and coming to a halt, my trumpeter sounded a parley. It was some time before I was attended to; and it was a feeling between awkwardness and irritation that was at last relieved by the approach of an officer, the "Mayor de Plaza;" and he again went into the palace and returned, before he was ready to conduct me thither.

I entered from the hall, a large and lofty apartment, with a carpeted earth floor, and discovered the governor seated at a table, with six or eight military and civil officials standing. There was no mistaking the governor, a large fine looking man, although his complexion was a shade or two darker than the dubious and varying Spanish; he wore a blue frock coat, with a rolling collar and a general's shoulder straps, blue striped trowsers with gold lace, and a red sash. He rose when I was presented to him; I said I was sent to him by the general commanding the American army; and that I had a letter, which I would present at his convenience. He said he had ordered quarters for me, and that my horses should be grazed near the town, by his soldiers, there being no corn; he hoped I would remain as long as it pleased me. I then took my leave. I was conducted by Captain Ortiz, Mayor de Plaza, to his quarters, and shown into a large long room, looking upon the court, and told "it was mine;" which truly Spanish politeness was belied soon after by the presence of Señor Gonzales: the room was carpeted, had one rude window, but a dozen, at least, of mirrors—a prevailing New Mexican taste,—and besides the divan, an American bedstead and bed. My men were rather crowded in a small room, on the opposite side of the narrow street, and to show my confidence, the horses were delivered to the Mexican soldier, to be grazed. Immediately a number of American merchants called on me; chocolate and cake, and some whiskey was handed round by the captain's wife.

Soon after, I went with an interpreter, for my official visit to the Governor, and delivered my credentials. He seemed to think that the approach of the army was rather sudden and rapid; and inquired very particularly if its commander, Kearny, was a general or colonel? (he had received his promotion on the march.) This was evidently to assist his judgment as to the strength of his force; and to follow the Napoleon maxim, to exaggerate the numbers of an army for its moral influence upon the enemy, our government would do well to take the hint; it being somewhat chary of that rank.

I was allowed to walk about the town; and I observed particularly the amount and condition of the ordnance.

Still sick, I had no appetite for dinner, and was disturbed at siesta, by a favorite trumpeter, who contrived to get admittance, and with much mystery of manner, gave me his opinion that a plan or determination had been formed by the soldiers to massacre or attack us in the night; I reassured him to the extent, that sobriety and prudence should not be lost sight of.

Señor Gonzales soon after raised his head from a table and in solemn, *not* sober voice, cried out " Cuchillo, Cuchara,—plata;" when, presto, appeared knives, spoons, plates;—mutton chops, chicken and chilo, tortillas, dulces, tea—whiskey. I could not eat the supper, but drew near the table, to please the Señora. The Don seized two ribs, and tearing them apart, sank his grizzly muzzle between. "*Un tena-dor*," I cried, mimicking the Don. The fork was brought, but the Don did not take hints then;—La Señora, offered me tea and cake on a silver salver. The Don poured whiskey into a bowl with his tea; and thinking I could put him to sleep, I helped him to more; he soon tumbled on his pallet, and saluted my ears with such horrid sounds that I fancied suffocation and explosion were contending for the mastery over his mountain of flesh.

At 10 P. M., General Armijo came with Don Santiago. It was settled that a "commissioner" should return with me, and that we should set out at sunrise; the Governor would march next day "with six thousand men." I promised to take chocolate with him at that early hour.

Accordingly on the 13th, soon after the sun rose, being all ready to mount, I paid my parting visit to Governor Armijo, when chocolate, cake and bread, —such as only Mexicans or Spaniards can make, —were served on silver plate; it is an article of my culinary creed, that only the Spanish, and their cognate tribes can make chocolate!

I do not go so far in the matter of bread; but

will state that notwithstanding there is not a bolting cloth in the province, their bread and cake cannot be excelled. But meanwhile the Governor is bowing me out, with a suspiciously good-humored smile, and deafening trumpets and drums seem beating to arms. I mount and ride forth, with my escort in compact order; and I pass that same guard-house, and hear the same sullen howl of the sentinel, which I still misunderstand; and rising in my stirrups I turn and with a defiant gesture, call out, in good English, " I'll call again in a week."

General Armijo, with little or no military experience, distrustful of the loyalty of the population he has habitually fleeced, and of their feeble ignorance which has been much impressed by our long commercial intercourse, is said to be in painful doubt and irresolution; halting between loyalty to his army commission, lately bestowed, and a desire to escape the dangers of war upon terms of personal advantage. Although perhaps much superior to those about him, he is unequal to the trying circumstances of his present situation. Even the patriotic spirit developed by his proclamation appears to embarrass as well as surprise him. Undoubtedly he must go on to direct this current, but to some weak and disgraceful conclusion. And Armijo's avarice, fortified by ignorance, probably excites in him some hope to handle the tariff dues of the large caravans which follow our column of invasion—an incident of war, strange to us, which must mystify him;—and it is a surprising fact that nearly all the merchants would prefer to get their clearances here; for three-fourths of their goods, in original packages, are destined for Chihuahua and even beyond; the Santa Fè custom house is a great favorite with them. Thus an almost prohibitory tariff, evaded by bribery, costs the people some thousand or two miles of land transportation; and thus a bad, corrupt government finds its account in abuses.

I was accompanied on my return by the "Commissioner," Dr. Conolly, an Englishman.

The second afternoon we passed the scene of a very recent murder and robbery; the Indians, as usual, are excited by the prospect of war, and the poor territory, never in the least protected by the handful of regulars at the capital, is now harried by these savages with unusual severity. My dragoons were chiefly intended for protection against them;

they, and not the New Mexicans, seem to be considered as our enemies.

Next morning, hearing of the approach of the army, I left my escort to rest their horses at the spring where we had slept, rode on, and was soon gladdened at sight of it, descending in gallant array the long hill to Tecolote.

There a halt was made. The General and suit were conducted by the alcalde to his house; and there, through his interpreter, General Kearny addressed him and the village notables; informing them of the annexation and its great advantages to them. He required the alcalde to take the oath of allegiance, and then confirmed him in his office, and pronounced them all released from their allegiance to Mexico, and citizens of the United States.

The march was then continued—the business with the alcalde having occupied only the space of time necessary for watering the horses, and the camp was established for the night at Bernal Spring.

My diary adds no word of comment! What a triumph of discipline!—I dismissed, as in a parenthesis, this accompaniment of a water-call. The great boon of American citizenship thus thrust, through an interpreter, by the mailed hand, upon eighty thousand mongrels who cannot read,—who are almost heathens,—the great mass reared in real slavery, called peonism, but still imbued by nature with enough patriotism to resent this outrage of being forced to swear an alien allegiance, by an officer who had just passed their frontier. This people who have been taught more respect for a corporal than a judge, must still have been astonished at this first lesson in liberty.

The General's authority for this course has no ampler record than may be found in the following extracts from confidential instructions received from the Secretary of War, and dated June 3d, 1846. "Should you conquer and take possession of New Mexico and Upper California, you will establish temporary civil governments therein, abolishing all arbitrary restrictions that may exist, so far as it may be done with safety. In performing this duty it would be wise and prudent to continue in their employment all such of the existing officers as are known to be friendly to the United States, and will take the oath of allegiance to them. . . . You may assure the people of those provinces that it is the wish and design of the United States to provide for them a free government, with the least possible delay, similar to that which exists in our Territories. They will then be called on to exercise the rights of freemen in electing their own representatives to the territorial legislature. It is foreseen that what relates to the civil government will be a difficult and unpleasant part of your duty, and much must necessarily be left to your own discretion.

"In your whole conduct you will act in such a manner as best to conciliate the inhabitants, and render them friendly to the United States."

Mr. Marcy also states, "No proclamation for circulation was ever furnished to General Kearny."

These instructions are the production of a politician and a lawyer; and it is necessary to add that their consummate author was well acquainted with Gen. Kearny.

The President, in communicating the above to Congress, said, "If any excess of power has been exercised, the departure has been the offspring of a patriotic desire to give to the inhabitants the privileges and immunities so cherished by the people of our own country. . . . Any such excess has resulted in no practical injury, but can and will be early corrected, in a manner to alienate as little as possible the good feelings of the inhabitants of the conquered territory." (December 22, 1846.)

The next day, with only a short halt of the column, a similar scene was enacted at San Miguel. I remained in town with a squadron; there was a great crowd; the General and his staff, the alcalde and a priest and a few others, ascended a flat house top overlooking the plaza; the General, through his interpreter, delivered his address with the advantage of its success at Tecolote, but, whether from the priest's influence, the crowd, or his own peculiar firmness, the alcalde positively refused to take the oath. The General then enlarged upon the perfect freedom of religion under our government, —mentioning that his chief of staff, then present, was a Roman Catholic. All persuasion failed, and at last the old man was forced to go through the form and semblance of swearing allegiance.

The army's second camp beyond San Miguel was on the hills of Pecos River, close to the ruins of the ancient temple, and of the church. That day General Armijo was posted at the defile, a very few miles beyond, with all his artillery, and a vast crowd of enemies.

The army marched very early August 18th; I commanded the advance guard, and held to the main road, not receiving orders to take the obscure route, known by the General, which turned the position at the cañon. As I passed it, I concluded that important information had been received in the night. So it proved, and I found at the rocky gorge only a rude breastwork of large trees felled across it. It had evidently proved impossible to give coherence to the wretched mass of our opponents, who were now for the first time assembled together.

They became panic-stricken at once on the approach of such an imposing array of horsemen of a superior race, and, it appeared, over-estimated our numbers, which the reports of ignorance and fear had vastly magnified.

Want of water compelled the extraordinary march of twenty-eight miles, and the arrival before Santa Fè near sundown. The dragoons were there alone, for a time, then came the regiment of volunteer cavalry; and the town had been summoned before the arrival of the artillery. Then we marched into the city, raised and saluted the national flag in the plaza, and marched back to make camp on the barren hill top. The baggage had not arrived; there were no provisions, no grass or other forage, no fuel; as a conquering army we fared badly. Before it was dark, the inhabitants were driving donkeys into camp loaded with fuel, and not long after the train came up; very few rations did it contain.

I took charge of the city for the night, with a guard of only fifty men; the General sleeping on the floor in the palace. The taverns and saloons were overrun by the hungry and thirsty volunteers, and at last I had to drive them all out. After midnight I lay down in my cloak in the main hall, or passage of the "palace," and there, with my saddle for a pillow, slept soundly.

The "Army of the West" marched from Bent's Fort with only rations calculated to last, by uninterrupted and most rapid marches, until it should arrive at Santa Fè. Is this war? Tested by the rules of the science, this expedition is anomalous, not to say Quixotic. A colonel's command, called an army, marches eight hundred miles beyond its base, its communication liable to be cut off by the slightest effort of the enemy—mostly through a desert—the whole distance almost totally destitute of resources, to conquer a territory of 250,000 square miles; without a military chest, the people of this territory are declared citizens of the United States, and the invaders are thus debarred the rights of war to seize needful supplies; they arrive without food before the capital—a city two hundred and forty years old, habitually garrisoned by regular troops! I much doubt if any officer of rank, but Stephen W. Kearny, would have undertaken the enterprise; or, if induced to do so, would have accomplished it successfully.

This is the art of war as practiced in America.

The horses were sent the day after our occupation of Santa Fè to a distant grazing camp, and the greater part of the troops were quartered in the town. The Indians have been coming in, and seem pleased at the new order of things; temporary civil officers have been sworn in. The authorities of Taos have submitted, and the prefect taken the oath of allegiance. Some of the civilized or "Pueblo" Indians from that quarter have visited us. These are a remarkable element in the New Mexican population. They are of the full blood, live in villages of houses of many stories, without doors—entered each story from its top, which is reached by a movable ladder: their diligently cultivated grounds they hold in fee; they speak the Spanish, besides an original language; comparatively moral, they profess the Roman Catholic religion, slightly modified by some cherished heathen customs and ceremonies, but are reputed far more moral christians than the New Mexicans proper, that is, of mixed blood; of these, the priests being preëminent scoundrels, their flocks are generally earnest in an imitation, where their inferior means and abilities do not admit of a possible success.

The market is well supplied; mutton of true mountain flavor, red peppers, onions, apples, apricots, etc. Coffee is fifty, and sugar forty cents a pound. Fandangos of the lowest class are now a great success.

Four of us have taken possession, temporarily, of the large parlor at my old quarters with the "Mayor de Plaza;" the captain has very quietly subsided into a civic character—that of vendor of El Paso wine and aguadiente, or brandy. All but some of our elderly officers take to a smattering of the Spanish, perhaps the easiest of languages to learn. This may account in part for its prevalence, to a convenient extent at least, even among the wild Indians within the sphere of Spanish conquest. First our men learned to ask, *leche de vaca, leche de cabra?* of the milk boys: goat's milk is far the more common, but is not popular with us.

A slave of the house, a captive when young from the Utah tribe, makes down every night our pallet beds. Major — is particular; and his persistence in minute directions to the girl, in very voluble English, of which she comprehends not one word, is so ludicrous, that our respectful attempts to smother our mirth usually result in a grand explosion. The major then, quite red in the face, laughs in a minor key.

Armi o on his retreat, dispersed the militia, and took with him the few regular troops, save some deserters. He had to abandon his artillery; and it has been all found and brought to the city: there are nine pieces; one is marked, "Barcelona, 1778."

A small fort is to be immediately commenced, on a hill which commands the town.

The great square or plaza, level, unpaved and rather sandy, has on each side a zequia, or canal, with rows of small cottonwood trees; this has a very pleasing effect in a hot, dry, and barren country. It is farther adorned with very comfortable porticoes,—*portales*,—on three sides, including the palace; these are extensions of the flat roofs to the edge of the side-walk, where they are supported by round pillars, which are whitewashed; they serve as the only shelter for the market; and are lined with shops, nearly all kept by Americans. One or two streets are similarly improved, but in general they are narrow and present to the passenger only a plain and nearly continuous wall; each extensive house having only a large strong folding door, and one or two windows; these have invariably a projecting frame and turned wooden bars; a sash seldom glazed—strong shutters opening inwards.

On our first Sunday the bells invited us to worship. I went to the parochial church: although built of adobes, it is sufficiently lofty, and has two steeples, or towers, in which hang three or four bells. With the usual wax images, it is adorned with numerous paintings—one or two of some merit. There was some music, of violin and triangle, and no spoken service. The streets and shops were thronged, and nothing indicated there that it was the Lord's day.

The General has issued a proclamation denouncing the penalties of treason against any found in hostility, in the Territory of New Mexico. He has directed the laws and decrees here found existing to be translated by Captain Waldo, Missouri Volunteers, with a view to their revision.*

After the full submission of the territory, and the

* The patient reader of these dry details and descriptions, which largely share the dullness of almost all realities, who looks out hopefully for some scintillations of humor as a merited relief, will sympathise with me in the loss of Don Santiago; but in bidding him farewell, I will incur the guilt of an anachronism, by giving you here a characteristic trait or two, in exigencies which soon befell him, as they will do, the most common and prosaic mortals. He got authority, as soon as we arrived, to push on with his friend and faithful imitator, Gonzales, to Chihuahua, he being in fact a habitant of that state (perhaps, indeed he was *sent*).

There arrived, Gonzales *was* soon sent to calaboose, for rehearsing in his cups, the Don's mountain speech, as was predicted; but Magoffin too, was incarcerated, as a *spy*: his life was really long in danger; but I am happy to record that he managed to dissolve all charges, prosecutions and enmities in three thousand three hundred and ninety two bottles of champagne wine ; (by a close computation,) and he lived to be remunerated by our government, as I particularly know. But the secretary said to him, mildly, "Mr. M. ten thousand dollars is a very large item for wine." "Yes," responded the Don with gravity, "but Mr. Secretary, champagne at $37.50 a basket counts up very fast." Try it yourself!

appointment of a temporary government, it becomes Gen. Kearny's duty to march for California, with such available force as he may judge requisite, to repeat the same rather dramatic exploits. New Mexico has furnished the scene of a good rehearsal at the least.

With this view the additional regiment and battalion were ordered; and these reënforcements, are supposed to be now well on their march.

Capt. A. R. Johnston, A. D. C. has been especially charged with the important subject of routes to California; two are represented as probably practicable; the more northern by the "old Spanish trail," which appears on some maps—and was suggested by the Secretary of War; Green River, and a sand desert of ninety miles are considered its great obstacles; and unless the reënforcements arrive soon, difficulty from snow is also apprehended. The second route by the river Gila is perhaps less known, but is pronounced to be too broken and mountainous for wagons, but to have more grass.

August 28th.—The General has decided to send a second column by the southern route; leaving the Rio Grande about one hundred and fifty miles below, and thence by the Rio Gila; this is certainly impracticable for wagons. The probability that the Gila will become our national boundary, and reports of Aztec ruins, give great interest to this expedition. Captain Cooke has been selected to command it.

The fact that the Spaniards, in their northern explorations, found here an isolated race quite advanced in civilization, compared to some tribes to its south, might prove an interesting study; that it is a fact, there is still existing proof enough, besides the name, New Mexico; it is kindred to the question of Aztec civilization.

Was that an original civilization? A tradition is reported by their conquerors that points to an European origin. It is well known that our continent was discovered and repeatedly visited about A.D. 1000 by Norsemen; *c'est le premier pas qui coute;* what more probable than that such adventurers should be attracted, step by step, toward a more genial, and to them a stranger clime!—should have coasted as far as Mexico,—beyond their power of return;—to communicate to an ingenuous race, their own moderate stock of knowledge and civilized arts; and especially that remarkably accurate astronomical knowledge of time, which may well be ascribed to navigators. Gradually absorbed, in five hundred years, should we not look for just the traces which were found, viz., an improved physical race;—sensible progress in art and social science;—and a tradition.

General Kearny has reported to the Secretary of War, that he has written to General Wool, directed to Chihuahua, that his expected reënforcements promise to be more than needed, in which case he will order a regiment South to report to him; and should General Wool not need them, he can order them on to General Taylor.

The Navajos, the Spanish spelling of their name, which is pronounced Navaho, are a numerous, and warlike tribe who dwell in fastnesses of the mountains westward of the Del Norte; they have advanced few of the usual first steps of civilization, and therefore very remarkably as manufacturers; for they make ponchôs, a blanket and blanket shawl, with a slit in the middle for the insertion of the head. Besides being waterproof, they are handsome, some of them approaching the India shawl in beauty and costliness. In fact the Navajos are richer than the mass of the people, whose flocks and herdsmen they harry; they have repressed their progress and lived on their spoil; the inhabitants have even been restrained by the government from making war upon them, except by special permission; and it is charged that Armijo used them as an effectual check to any resistance to his arbitrary oppressions.

The influence of the Spanish protection of this and the neighboring provinces against unconquered Indian tribes, began to cease about the year 1832; and from that date they have decayed; it is estimated that the number of sheep is eighty per cent less than then. I am assured that one man has lost 250,000! The people are almost confined to villages.

Except in narrow valleys and narrow strips, mostly wooded, reached by mountain showers, the whole province, alluvion as well as table-land, is so arid as to *seem* uninhabitable. There is some rain, but an elevation of from four thousand to seven thousand feet, and the absence of forests and even groves, make it almost nugatory. Irrigation is necessary in the river lands, and is effectual, where practicable, on the hills.

There are, indeed, the mile or two wide river bottoms of the Rio Abajo, (lower river,) of only four to five thousand feet elevation, which although very sandy, are quite productive, and of charming climate; but the want of fuel makes even that best district unattractive. Thus any considerable immigration cannot be expected.

It should not be omitted that the precious metals have been long known to be very diffusely found here; but no one seems ever to have made a fortune in the mines. A pains-taking culture by irrigation, and sheep pastures, are the main supports of a sparse population in New Mexico.

They make sugar, from the corn-stalk; butter—rather a test of civilization—scarcely any; no oats or rye are produced, few potatoes; onions, very fine, and chile Colorado, are the chief vegetables; melons are plenty.

Yesterday the 27th, the General, or Governor, gave a ball to all the officers, and to citizens generally in the government house; it was a political, or conciliatory affair, and we put the best face on it. The women are comely,—remarkable for smallness of hands and feet: as usual in such states of society, they seem superior to the man; but nowhere else is chastity less valued or expected.

There was an attempt at cotilions; but the natives are very Germans for waltzing—and they possess musical ears as well. Their favorite, called appropriately the cuna (cradle) is peculiar; it is a waltz; but the couple stand face to face; the gentleman encircles his partner's waist with both arms; the lady's similarly disposed, complete the sides of the cradle which is not bottomless, for both parties lean well back as they swing around. There were men present in colored cotton trowsers secured by leathern belts, and jackets, but they danced well. The American merchants were of course, very genteelly represented; there were twenty or thirty of them. The supper was good, particularly in cake. The fiddlers accompanied their music at times by verses, sung in a high nasal key. I was surprised, but amused to hear one of our captains join in this; —and he could waltz them all blind;—but we got him from the navy.

The ball went off harmoniously, and quite pleasantly, considering the extravagant variety in its make up. But we did not feel particular—out here.

August 31*st.*—A report is believed that a Colonel

Ugarte is entering the southern extremity of the territory with some five hundred regulars, to meet and re-inforce General Armijo; this must hasten the march south, which has been announced.

Four hundred wagons of supplies have been reported on the way out—as also Colonel Price's regiment.

The greatest expense of this invasion, possibly, will be found in the matter of transportation. The territory seems quite unequal to feed its seventeen hundred conquerors; they have received for weeks but nine ounces of ground wheat per day, and no sugar or coffee! The men must make out a living from other resources;—but they receive no pay, and scurvy is making its appearance.

I marched from Santa Fè yesterday with half of my dragoons, afoot, twenty-six miles;—seeking to establish a grazing camp on the Galisteo. After leaving the zequias, which invade for several miles the gravelly table land, we were without water for near twenty, and the camp is a mile from grass. The ox teams with baggage lately arrived from Missouri, set out half a day in advance, but did not come up, and so we bivouacked; after a hot day, the night being rather frosty, I caught a slight cold. It is a healthy country, but catarrhs and pleurisy are not uncommon.

September 1st.—Last night an officer came for dragoons to man a battery of four howitzers, and with an order to hold myself ready—until farther orders—to march south at an hour's notice; the General having received some confirmation of the junction of Armijo and Ugarte; we are also to move over to the main southern road to-morrow.

September 2d.—We marched, accordingly, eighteen miles, leaving the nearly dry Galisteo for the table land. In a vale at noon, finding some grass, although there was no water, I stopped an hour to graze; this on Dugald Dalgetty's principle, which in this country must be applied to horses and mules. Approaching the Rio Grande we came to the broken descent of a small stream, and a rancho; a few cottonwoods or poplars added much attraction to its appearance,—so rare is this only " ornamental " tree; and we saw the dust of the mile long column of the General's march toward the south.

The little valley of this farm-house looked quite green; but, as usual, the grass had been closely cropped; one of the merchants bound for Chihuahua —they are all still involuntary Micawbers—having here established his caravan; his mules contended with the farmer's sheep, asses and goats for a subsistence.

And so we camped a mile further, on the dusty upland where we found scant buffalo grass and that called grama.

Professor Torrey seems to have pronounced buffalo grass "polygamous by abortion;" the phrase, if possible to be understood, referring to his belief that its flower is not fertile. But I have gathered much of its fruit—like large grains of oats truncated. But I have also seen, with the pregnant *if*, that I could believe my eyes, the buffalo and the grama, so very different in most respects, growing from the same root! if that constitutes vegetable polygamy; but they are the very same in being frost-proof and good substantial food for the granivora.

The baggage wagons having gone astray, we had until after dark a prospect of being supperless and shelterless, even without fires; for it is by many expedients that we manage to have fuel, even for cooking.

A message from the General sets at rest, as unfounded, the prospect of hostilities further south. Colonel Ugarte did march over the border; and if Armijo had proved a good soldier, our conquest might well have furnished better elements for an epic. We are commanded to devote ourselves to preparing the horses for the California expedition.

September 4th.—Yesterday the General left his column and baggage and turned aside, escorted by a squadron of dragoons, to visit the Pueblo Indian town of Santo Domingo, having been invited to do so, several days ago. Not having been present, I will give a picturesque description of the visit, by a staff officer, the more interesting as concerning this tribe without the pale of citizenship, but more moral, and superior in some other respects to the mass of the people; their extraordinary abstinence from mixture of blood reminds one of the Jews.

He writes: "From height to height, as we advanced, we saw horsemen disappearing at full speed. As we arrived abreast of the town, we were shown, by the guard, posted for the purpose, the road to Santo Domingo. * * We had not proceeded far, before we met ten or fifteen sachemic looking old Indians, well mounted, two of them carrying gold-headed canes with tassels, the emblems of office in New Mexico.

Salutations over, we jogged along, and in the course of conversation, the alcalde, a grave and majestic old Indian, said, as if casually, "We shall meet some Indians presently, mounted and dressed for war, but they are the young men of my town, friends, come to receive you, and I wish you to caution your men not to fire upon them when they ride towards them."

When within a few miles of the town, we saw a cloud of dust rapidly advancing, and soon the air was rent with a terrible yell, resembling the Florida war-whoop. The first object that caught my eye through the column of dust, was a fierce pair of buffalo horns, overlapped with long shaggy hair. As they approached, the sturdy form of a naked Indian revealed itself beneath the horns, with shield and lance, dashing at full speed, on a white horse, which, like his body, was painted all the colors of the rainbow; and then, one by one his followers came on, painted to the eyes, their own heads and their horses, covered with all the strange equipments that the brute creation could afford in the way of horns, skulls, feathers, tails and claws.

As they passed us, one rank on each side, they fired a volley under our horses' bellies from the right and from the left. Our well-trained dragoons sat motionless on their horses, which went along without pricking an ear or showing any sign of excitement.

Arrived in the rear, the Indians circled round, dropped into a walk on our flanks until their horses recovered breath, when off they went at full speed passing to our front, and when there, the opposite files met, and each man selected his adversary and kept up a running fight, with muskets, lances, and bows and arrows. Sometimes a fellow would stoop almost to the earth to shoot under his horse's belly, at full speed, or to shield himself from an impending blow. So they continued to pass and repass all the way to the steep cliff which overhangs the town. There they filed on each side of the road, which descends through a deep cañon, and halted on the peaks of the cliffs. Their motionless forms projected against the clear blue sky above, formed studies for an artist. In the cañon we were joined by the priest, a fat old white man. We were escorted first to the padre's, of course; for here, as everywhere, these men are the most intelligent, and the best to do in the world, and when the good people wish to put their best foot foremost, the padre's wines, beds, and couches have to suffer. The entrance to the portal was lined with the women of the village, all dressed alike, and ranged in treble files; they looked fat and stupid.

We were shown into his reverence's parlor, tapestried with curtains stamped with the likenesses of all the Presidents of the United States up to this time. The cushions were of spotless damask, and the couch covered with a white Navajo blanket, worked in richly colored flowers.

The air was redolent with the perfume of grapes and melons, and every crack of door and windows glistening with the bright eyes and arms of the women of the capilla. The old priest was busy talking in the corner, and little did he know the game of sighs and signs carried on between the young fellows and the fair inmates of the house. We had our gayest array of young men out to-day, and the women seemed to me to drop their usual subdued look and timid wave of the eye-lash for good hearty twinkles and signs of unaffected and cordial welcome—signs supplying the place of conversation, as neither party could speak the language of the other. This little exchange of the artillery of eyes was amusing enough, but I was very glad to see the padre move towards the table, and remove the pure white napkin from the grapes, melons and wine. We were as thirsty as heat and dust could make us, and we relished the wine highly, whatever its quality. The sponge cake was irreproachable, and would have done honor to our best northern house-keepers. Indeed, wherever we have feasted, the sponge cake has been in profusion, and of the best kind. After the repast, the General went forward on the portal and delivered a speech to the assembled people of the town, which was first interpreted into Spanish, and then into Pueblo.

It is impossible to arrive at the precise population of the town, but I should judge it to be about six hundred, and the quantity of ground under tillage for their support about five hundred acres. Six miles lower they passed San Felippe, " suggesting pictures we sëe of castles on the Rhine."

We marched yesterday toward Santa Fè in search of grass ; winding among the hills we passed several spring branches ; making inquiries at the houses, the people were evidently averse to our stopping, regarding us perhaps, in the light of a swarm of locusts; and so, there was generally good grass several miles further on ; they object to selling the green corn. Camp at last was established twelve miles from the city, in a long strip of green meadow, clipped indeed, but making a pleasant camp. A sod for the floor of a tent is here a luxury.

September 5*th*.—Making a virtue of necessity, or really having a surplus, the small farmers begin to sell their patches of corn ; it is cut at the root, brought in wagons to camp, and fed at night to horses, ear, blade and stalk ; and there is not a particle of litter in the morning. The poor horses are taken about nine o'clock, several miles, to graze on the scant grass of the upland, where there is no water, and are brought in at three o'clock. It is not a pleasant duty to herd them on a bare prairie six or seven hours, through the heat of the day ; there was a little rain this afternoon.

Near us is a house prettily situated on a point

of hill overlooking corn fields; but its chief beauty is a small grove of cottonwoods; the little fields fill the irregular valleys, and are without fences; even here they are irrigated; the soil, of hill or table land and valley is nearly the same; the high ground near Santa Fè is in cultivation.

The sheep here are very small, the wool quite coarse; but the flesh is of excellent flavor. The wool, without a market, is used for mattresses, which are very well made and comfortable, and for carpets and packing blankets.

To the philosophic observer of the infinitely wise adaptations throughout Nature, it is not surprising that in those portions of our earth rendered barren by elevation, want of rain and excessive evaporation, there is always found a configuration which makes irrigation easy and suggests it. I have seen, in Utah, an irrigating ditch, on upland, straight for miles!—I have pronounced ground of gravel and sand, producing nothing but a few stunted weeds of one species, as utterly worthless,—and afterward beheld it green with almost tropical profusion,—its latent germs vivified by water.

The few rich men live in the Rio Abajo; their

extensive plastered and whitewashed residences, built around large courts, are quite imposing; and each contains, the key of their wealth, a store of necessaries for their dependent laborers. This is the system of peonage; at their own prices they manage to keep the poor peons always in debt, and this legally binds them and their families to endless service and dependence; and they can be cast off, without any provision in their old age. They have been informed that they shall soon have a voice in their own government. Doubtless this flagrant servitude will be gradually broken up; but when shall such people be capable of self-government! There will be a territorial government for thirty years*—and the language will not change faster than the color of the citizens.

All the advantages seem to be with the conquered. What for us? except the convenience of a rounded boundary; it is not the route to California; these routes will be above or below.* The proclamation of Governor Kearny " announces his intention to hold the Department with its original boundaries [on both sides of the Del Norte] as a part of

---

* These words were written Sept. 5th, 1846.

the United States, and under the name of the Territory of New Mexico."

This overleaps the first announcement which seemed the assertion of the old Texan claim.

The Mormon Battalion is now not expected before October, that will be too late for the northern route to California; and the last information seems to make that by the Gila River impracticable for want of grass, if at all practicable for wagons. And so there would remain only a long route through Sonora. Evidence is all doubtful or false;—false wilfully, or only from lack of judgment as to the needs of a large force compared to that of a few adventurers.

September 7th.—I visited Santa Fè yesterday; a tall, handsome flagstaff has just been erected in the plaza, conveying perhaps some idea of permanency to the ignorant people; while the fort on the hill begins to show itself to the town. Great complaint, however, is made that the volunteers will scarcely work; daily labor was not embraced in their conceptions of war; it goes some way to prove that democracy and discipline—of the military sort—are not entirely congenial. The fort is named Marcy, after the eminent statesman.

I visited to-day the house near camp,—of exceptional character and surroundings; a pleasant portal in front of a fine room, looks upon a small grove of well grown cottonwood trees; these deriving their verdure, or rather their existence, from a fast flowing spring in their midst. From the house we also see the rather narrow winding valley, highly cultivated, walled in by little rock precipices; there is, too, an ancient round tower of two floors,—the upper story of stone; it is loop-holed, and a stone wall crossing some low hills is very remarkable. The happy proprietor is a rather cultivated man; and his Spanish was pleasant to hear.

The country generally, off the river, is not appropriated in severalty. Colonel Doniphan, who is a lawyer of high repute, is codifying and revising the laws; he tells me of this, and many peculiar difficulties; the civil law as adopted by Spain is their basis; its adaptations are rather from many departmental decrees, than National legislation; and so low has been the state of administration of justice in this province, that suits of any importance have been removed seven or eight hundred miles to Chihuahua.

Our fuel is brought nine miles, and the nights

are very cold. This pure atmosphere has often a peculiar haze or blueness which is unaccounted for; the nearest mountains look dark blue, and when covered by cedars and pines, almost black.

September 11*th*.—I slept last night under a thick blanket and buffalo robe.

The Pueblos bring in for sale melons, onions, corn, sugar and molasses, bread, and above all, delicious grapes; they are as large as musket balls, the bunches of about a pound weight; in no other part of the world, as I think, are there grapes so palatable. The cultivation, and I am told it is the same in California, is peculiar; pruning is so extreme that the growth ceases to be a vine, and becomes a single stem four or five feet high, which supports the short branches and fruit: thus it is a bush. The wine they make here is not highly praised.

The General passed up this afternoon; the national flag is to be hoisted on the new staff, first in his presence, under a national salute.

Some of the staff tell us that their march was a gala procession, extending only ninety miles to San Tomè. They arrived there on their saint's day; long tallow candles were put into the hands of the officers to carry in procession, following his waxen effigy; and this was considerably protracted, by repeated addresses to his saintship. At night there were fireworks, rockets from doors and windows of the church, bonfires on the adobe turrets, etc. The village was crowded. Families journeyed in their primitive wagons, rough boxes on solid wooden wheels. Women came on donkeys and mules, on which last they invariably ride in front of men, who nevertheless hold the reins. There are few horses in the country.

The officers partook of a collation at the padre s. The ladies never made their appearance at the houses at which the general and officers were entertained; one of them at an accidental interview with an officer proved exceedingly inquisitive as to our country; when questioned as to Armijo, she abused him, and pointing to his shoulder straps, exclaimed, "I don't know how any man wearing these things could run away as he did; he had a good army to back him, and could have driven you all back."

The Navajos are continually making raids on these poor people; they seem to have had the policy to avoid utterly ruining them, and to leave them the means of increase for the perpetual enforcement of contributions. They have made irruptions within two or three miles of our troops. Protection has been promised, and even compensation for losses since our arrival.

September 22d.—Gen. Kearny approved and decreed an " organic law for the territory of New Mexico, in the United States of America;" it grants the electoral franchise to "all free male citizens of the territory;" and "the first election of a delegate to the Congress of the United States, and for members of the general assembly shall be on the first Monday in August, A. D. 1847." It comprises the usual "Bill of Rights," also "Laws for the government of the territory," including all details of administration, in the judicial, and every other department ;—revenue, registry of lands, costs, fees, fines, etc., etc.

The same day, "being duly authorized by the President," etc., he appointed Charles Bent to be Governor; also a secretary, marshal, U. S. district attorney, (Francis P. Blair); a treasurer, auditor, and three judges of the superior court.

September 23d.—There is no mail to the States, and no established communication; but Col. Price's regiment is known to be well advanced on his march; and Colonel Doniphan's regiment is to-day ordered, when relieved by Price's, to march to Chihuahua. Captain Hudson of Doniphan's, has been ordered to organize a troop of one hundred men, who will volunteer from that regiment, to be mounted on mules to accompany the Mormon battalion to California.

(Capt. H. failed to raise the troop; the result of a want of specie, and other difficulty in procuring their mount.)

Our horses have become poorer, notwithstanding all efforts to recruit them by all means available.

The days are still hot; we were told on our arrival, August 18, that the rainy season had begun about a week before, and that it lasted two or three weeks; but a gentle sprinkle of the mountain showers reaches us now, nearly every day.

This country is nearly destitute of game. Prairie-dog villages are common, and there is one actually joining my camp; the dogs are not molested, and are very tame. I suppose them to be the most numerous mammals of North America; we find their " towns " spread all over the high and dry regions; they live on the roots and blades of the grama grasses; and seem to require no water.

The southern promontory of the Rocky Mountains, which overlooks Santa Fè, is now white with snow.

September 25*th.*—To-morrow is now set for the beginning of our venturesome expedition through the unknown wilderness of mountains and dry plains to the Pacific Ocean; we have had a boisterous, rainy night, our first.

Nothing is heard of the war in Mexico; our position here has been unfortunate, irksome, disheartening—so far from the "sabre clash" of the sunny South! Truly there is a "Fortune of War;" and the pedestal of the goddess is Opportunity! That a soldier should pass through a war without distinction I used to think—and does not the world?—is to be set down to his fault or want of merit. But how near were some of us to being excluded from all action, and in spite of our vehement applications; and how much resignation to the consciousness of mere duty performéd, is the only support of our obscure lot, in this field of war's drudgery!

"The world"—which means that average mass of low grade in intelligence and information, and absorbed, following the law of their natures, in the small but important interests of self,—is only reached by the most brilliant and striking actions, or by long continued great prominence of action. Working in this obscurity, our most faithful, venturous, long-continued labors, amid all privations and exposures, fruitful though they prove to be in the annexation of imperial extents of territory, conquering Nature itself in its most naked and forbidding shapes, shall be ignorantly accepted—placed in the appendix, as it were, of history. Momentary actions, of excitement so exhilarating as to exclude the thought of danger, shall receive the shouts of crowds, the applause of the nation; and history shall eloquently record the success of deeds resulting from some obscure inspiration, some subordinate act. But the working out shall be done by the heroic rank and file, of whom so many shall moulder in unknown trenches, named only in company records.

To-morrow, three hundred wilderness-worn dragoons, in shabby and patched clothing, who have long been on short allowance of food, set forth to conquer or "annex" a Pacific empire; to take a leap in the dark of a thousand miles of wild plains and mountains, only known in vague reports as unwatered, and with several deserts of two and three marches where a camel might starve if not perish of thirst.

Our success—we never doubt it! and the very desperation of any alternative must ensure it—shall give us for boundary, that world line of a mighty ocean's coast, looking across to the cradle land of humanity; and shall girdle the earth with civilization. Then, will *one* name be added to the roll of fame? A single dash on a blazing battery shall win more applause, and more reward.

We are haunted by the ghostly shapes of our starving horses. To this camp where they were tied up on bare sand—escaping their guards who are to drive them to Missouri,—passing by fenceless corn-fields; here, as if to make dumb reproach for ingratitude—to forbid this severance of old association, they come threading their way by day and by night through the tents; their gaunt shapes upbraid us, their sunken eyes make pathetic appeal. Some of them, to my knowledge, have served thirteen years; would it not be a consolation to inform them that their half-breed successors are chosen for a forlorn hope! But they are cast adrift as useless servants, to take a desperate journey of eight hundred miles, with grass for food, and much of that destroyed by frost. Farewell forever, old friends!

September 26th.—At 7.30 this morning began our first march; after the hot and dreary twenty-one miles of table land, we descended into the bottom land of El Rio Grande del Norte; here wholly ours, and its lower course illustrated by our arms, this name can no more swell pleasantly on the tongue of the Mexican.

The camp is on a zequia; and so far from its source, that its bottom is above the camp; and close beyond is a lower one; the fields of maize are near. This mile wide savanna, not too sandy to be very green, I have no doubt was charming to the eyes of our mules,—fasting and thirsting, through a long day of toil; but for them, it is very like seating a famishing man to the dessert of a vanished dinner. Well in truth the comparison is not far-fetched;—for our sole fuel is some cedar boughs we gathered while passing the Galisteo, and the Pueblos from San Domingo have extemporized a very fair market in our camp. They bring only fruit, melons, peaches, and the delightful grapes. I should not omit the onions, for they are truly the finest in the world, and—can be eaten raw.

September 27th.—A day of small mishaps, beginning with a provoking but most lively mule adventure. When the regiment was ready to march, a loose mule of my troop, dragging a long rope, had been pursued for an hour by several men; the march began, leaving me to send out my whole company to catch the perverse and most active beast; and it was actually another hour, the whole of them galloping around, assisted by numbers of Indians on foot, before we succeeded. Fourteen Indians were " in at the death ;" one remarkable fellow must have run about six miles.

Then I marched, and in a mile or two found my wagon with the pole broken short off, in passing one of the zequias with the usual troublesome steep banks; if it had been irreparable, it is hard to say what could have been done, with nothing but cottonwoods within a day's ride.

The bottom now expands, with pleasant groves

in view; it looks more like a habitable country. We passed several pueblos, and then Bernalillo, the prettiest village of the Territory. Its view, as we approached, was refreshing; green meadows, good square houses, and a church, cottonwoods, vineyards, orchards—these jealously walled in; and there were numbers of small fat horses grazing. The people seemed of superior class,—handsomer and cleaner. But parts of this bottom had sand hillocks, with their peculiar arid growths.

At another village I overtook the regiment, and brought it on, leaving the general and some others dining at an immense house owned by young Perea. I made camp seventeen miles from our last, near a village; the grass poor and thin, and no fuel. We have to make the best of weeds and chance fragments. The wagons came up at sunset, some of the mules already breaking down, from the heavy draught of sandy roads.

There are myriads of wild fowl—geese, brant, sand-cranes; the people seem never even to molest them!

For two days, continuing the march, great efforts have been made to exchange mules, evidently unfit for the expedition, for better, and also to make purchases. Approaching Albuquerque, I rode for miles as through a straggling village. At one of the Armijos I partook, with the General, of a collation of grapes, cakes, and syrup lemonade. The general quizzed a padre of the company, about the relations of the Mexican church with Rome; the padre contended that the suspended relations were the consequence solely of the revolution. I also dined there; the table service presented a mixture of silver gilt with tin and earthenware: we see also silver forks with the commonest bone-handled knives. A son of fifteen lately returned from college at St. Louis, Missouri, remarked he was going to Mexico to finish his education !

At Albuquerque we forded the river, which is about two feet deep and twenty-five yards wide; it is low, but does not rise more than two feet. This is several hundred miles from the sources of the river; but into the account of its swift flowing waters, several zequias should be taken, and these are eight to ten feet wide, and about two feet deep. We marched about seven miles down the river, through a sandy plain, without fuel, scarcely inhabited or cultivated, and camped at a zequia. We are opposite, it seems, a pass of the Navajos; and but a few days ago they made an irruption, killed several persons, and drove off about two thousand sheep.

The quarter-master has hired several wagons and teams to go a few marches, at eight dollars a day; only five dollars were demanded, if protected, in returning, against the Indians.

September 30*th*.—We pass to-day immense cornfields; the fruitfulness of the sandy soil is attributed to a gypsum ingredient; the common houses have window lights of its laminated crystals. We pass several handsome villages;—Padillas, Isletta. This last is a Pueblo, and is on a swell of the bottom, surrounded by green meadows, and sand hillocks. On the river we saw large groves;*—the vineyards are, as usual, protected by high adobe walls. I observed there a singular fashion of the women; the short skirts revealed the legs bandaged to an evidently unnatural size. But they were not destitute of beauty.

* If it were possible for the reader to put himself in full sympathy with any participator in the marches and explorations of this volume, he would not wonder at an unfailing and glad mention of any green thing,—especially those masterpieces of the vegetable kingdom, to wit, *trees*. Pleasing and strange to his eyes!—strong reminders of home! and, so suggestive of the infinite comfort of fuel!

After a black frost last night, the heat to-day was severe; we marched but thirteen miles; but were in all respects in miserable plight for such an expedition. We are endeavoring, as we go, to complete our outfit in *one* important particular,—that of mules.

October 1st.—Still warm weather and distressing dust. All the houses and villages we are now passing are adorned by cottonwood; but all the same, we are much straitened for fuel; I paid twenty-five cents for a small stick. The Quartermaster crossed over to Valencia this morning seeking mules; he should succeed there, for it is the residence of several nabobs; but it is disaffection as much as want of specie which prevents our supply; we should have dealt with a higher hand; campaigns cannot wait for the "inheritance" of meekness. At Valencia resides a Widow C., whose husband was murdered by Americans a few years ago; they went out, several hundred miles from Independence, Mo., to rob him, knowing he had with him a large sum; they murdered him in cold blood; and it is satisfactory to add, that they were hanged for it, at Saint Louis. The widow is fair and *firm*; for, *on dit*, she refuses to wed her companion, preferring to remain mistress of her very considerable wealth. Her house is said to be furnished splendidly.

October 2d.—Between the very decided descent of the valley, and our progress south, the days are hot. This morning we passed unusually thick settlements, and the large village of Savinal, with its handsome church, and unusually picturesque surroundings. Below there are very few houses; and after noon, we passed a vast baked plain, whitened by salts, with a burning sun overhead; our progress to-day was sixteen miles, and our camp is opposite La Joya de Ciboletta, the "jewel of a little bull," or "little buffalo;" I consider it an outlandish name; there must be a little tale to it, if one could only get hold of it; but perhaps, after all, it should be spelled Cebolletta; the little onion!

This camp has more variegated surroundings than any we have had; the scenery is pretty; it is on a bend of the river, which here has groves of cottonwoods; sand hills below us approach close to the river, on both sides, and shut up the valley. A very friendly mayor-domo of a neighboring ranche, has sent us word that forty of the Navajos passed the river last night; thus warning us to be watchful of our animals.

An express has arrived from Santa Fè; Colonel Price reports his arrival; he confirms the death of Colonel Allen of the Mormon Volunteers. And now, at night, I have been selected to succeed him; which, of course, must turn my face to Santa Fè to-morrow. That is turning a very sharp corner indeed; it is very military.; (but it is said to be a manœuvre not unknown to another profession.)

October 3d.—The camp is not moved to-day; a very remarkable thing for General Kearny; but the Mexican wagons, assisting transportation temporarily, had this time to be waited for. It happens very conveniently, as I have my company and property to deliver to my lieutenant; I am kindly allowed to keep three of my men, and shall leave two of them in this neighborhood in charge of my baggage, until my return.

And now comes a messenger with foaming steed; he tells of a village twelve miles below, Pulvidera, being attacked by Navajos, and a troop of dragoons is ordered to their relief.

Orders were sent to-day to Colonel Doniphan to

make a campaign against the Navajos before proceeding on his adventures to the South.

About noon, accompanied by my bugler, I left camp for Santa Fè. Near Savinal, I forded the river, being desirous of seeing the eastern side of the valley. I was told it was eight miles to San Tomè; two miles further on a villager informed me it was twelve miles from there; riding on several miles through fine meadows, a respectably dressed native told me it was just fifteen miles from there; several miles further I met a man on foot who assured me it was twenty miles; I had been all the time approaching the phantom village. Several miles further on, at dark, I came to the camp of a caravan merchant, who offered me supper; he informed me it was really six miles from there to Tomè; and so I found it, and without a house on the road. In the edge of the village however, some trees and a corn-field round a house, tempted me to seek lodgings there, as it was quite dark. The fellow opened the door, and the light, at sight of horsemen, was instantly blown out; he jerked out, like a pistol shot, "no hai" (there's nothing here). I could not at the moment make the allowance of his fright or fear, which was prudence in such a country, for the rudeness of his inhospitality: and so returned a bad word or two in bad Spanish, as I turned off to enter the town. There my wants were ministered to at the padre's. In some after supper chat, I discovered that my deficiency in Spanish could be helped out by some command of Latin words common to the priest and myself.

October 4th.—I arrived at breakfast time at the straggling village of Valencia, and went to the house of Señor Otero; one of the large residences here, which are unlike any European or American. You ride in at a great gate into a very spacious court, surrounded on four sides by apartments, store rooms, offices, provision for all the requirements of the family, the farm, and for trade; all one story, of thick plastered and whitewashed walls. It was Sunday morning: I encountered first an Indian slave woman, carrying to the chamber of a young man, on a silver salver, chocolate and sponge cake, which they take at rising; he was the store-keeper, and a Texan by birth; and such was my own introduction to a substantial breakfast, which came later.

I had some political chat with Señor Otero

who, like the few other men of large wealth was malcontent; they must dread, perhaps rather vaguely, the loss of their iniquitous privileges; but he discreetly vented his spleen on Armijo and his conduct which he regarded as disgraceful; and *professed* that he would have favored a voluntary annexation.

I wanted to get mules of Otero; his prices were exorbitant.

I rode here a small brown horse, with a Roman nose, that I think possessed the greatest virtues and vices of the horse and the ass, with a trace or two of the goat. Last year, on the last quarter of a two thousand mile ride, on poor grass, he resented a solitary application of spurs, by whirling around like a dancing dervish, making several goat leaps, and then prancing thirty miles;—put a severe bit on him, and he would run away. He was the best buffalo horse I ever rode; nervous to timidity, he would nevertheless carry you along side of the shaggiest monster of ten thousand rushing with a concussion to shake the earth, regardless of the polished tip of horn and the malignant black eye rolling toward him; only shrinking slightly with half averted head, in expectancy of the pistol shot; his motion all the while so steady you could adjust the nicest aim : and I have thus brought down, on him, a noble elk, surrounded by a forest of antlers, and to the music of a thousand hoofs ringing like castanets! Poor Brown!—Of all our enquiries, discussions, and doubts, as to our destined California "bourne," perhaps there has been but one agreed conclusion, viz : that no horse could reach it, much less "return." Well, I had set out with Bolinski, trusting in his virtues, or else, resigned to the worst that might befall his vices.

But this morning, although I was confident that he had hitherto tried and exercised my patience to virtuous perfection, in an unhappy moment, for both of us, perhaps, he outdid himself and patience. Approaching Otero's house, after a very free indulgence in eccentricities, he reached a crisis by trotting off, *backwards*, until we soused into a muddy and profound zequia. I swapped him to Otero, for a mule. Poor Bolinski!

Continuing my journey with my attendant, I arrived late, and spent the night at Señor Sandoval's, three miles below Albuquerque; this is another of the imposing feudal residences of this primitive society. And here I had the unhoped success of purchasing of Señor Sandoval twenty fine mules, to be delivered at Santa Fè, for one thousand dollars.

On the 5th, we lay at Algodones; on the 6th, at the picturesque rancho of Señor Vaca y Delgado, my old acquaintance, where I camped so long, and on the 7th reached Santa Fè.

The battalion had not arrived.

I find the quarter-master department without funds; and with much allowance for disaffection, and primitive ignorance, it is strange to add, with little credit. The principal capitalists of the territory are caravan merchants whose trade to the United States has been almost wholly balanced by specie, for which they have accepted bills of exchange.

The consequence seems almost fatal to my expedition. A reasonable anticipation of its difficulties demands a very careful and perfect outfit; and especially in the now scarce and very expensive article of draft mules.

It is interesting to read now from the Washington correspondence of a famous New York daily—dated July 3d, that "In the capture of the city of Santa Fè alone, it is estimated, that, if the movement is prompt and efficient, at least fifteen millions in specie and gold dust will be captured."

While thus waiting, I give the incidents which befell General Kearny's column before it passed beyond this valley and communications; the news of which has closely followed me.

The march was continued, October 4th, down the river. The succor of Pulvidera was too late to save a large amount of stock which the Navajos drove off; and the General then published *permission* to the people to retaliate, and make war upon the Navajos.

On the 5th the column reached Socorro;—where the guides had proposed to leave the river; but after much discussion, they changed their mind.

On the 6th they marched thirteen miles. This day Kit Carson with fifteen men,—an express from California—was met; he had an important mail for Washington.

The great news was a revolution or subjugation of California under the auspices of Commodore Stockton and Captain Fremont.

Six of Carson's party were Delawares; he started with fifty riding animals; the most of them had been ridden down and abandoned; others swapped, two for one, with Apaches, who proved friendly; he came by the Gila. No news of the invasion of New Mexico had been received in California.

General Kearny determined to take Carson to guide him by the route he had just passed over. Carson resisted very firmly, at first; he had pledged himself to deliver his mail in Washington. The General finally prevailed,—taking upon himself every responsibility,—especially the prompt and safe delivery of the dispatches.

Did the General stop to think what it was he demanded? A man had just ridden eight hundred miles over a desert,—a wilderness,—where he could meet no human being save a few savages likely to seek his destruction; (he rode ninety miles without halting, over a jornada of sand!) he had arrived at the verge of society, and *near the residence of his family!* He is required to turn right back, and for another year of absence! That was no common sacrifice to duty.

General Kearny then decided to take only two small troops of dragoons, as an escort, and also two mountain howitzers, sending back Major Sumner with four troops to remain in the territory. He then marched three days, with wagons, with eight picked mules to the wagon; but a day and a half without a road satisfied him; he sent for pack saddles, and gave up the wagons. October 14th, he once more resumed his march, and, next day being about two hundred and thirty miles below Santa Fè, he left the river, turned westward; toward the copper mines on the Gila, and wrote to Colonel Cooke, assigning to him the task of opening a wagon road to the Pacific.

Colonel Doniphan, in obedience to orders, leaving Colonel Price at Santa Fè, marched October 26th, against the Navajos. He directed one column of two hundred men under Major Gilpin up the Chama River. It went as far as the mountains dividing the waters of the Del Norte from those of the Colorado, thence down the San Juan, and by Red Lake to the valley of the Little Colorado.

With the remaining portion of the regiment he left the Rio Grande at Albuquerque, and passed up the valley of the Puerco, or Pecos of the West, almost to its source; in three parties he visited their whole country, and collected the most of the tribe at Bear Spring (Ojo del Oso) and made a treaty. The marches were over mountains, and generally in snow. The regiment was concentrated at Socorro, December 12th.

Colonel Doniphan's Capture of Chihuahua —A Brief Episode.

The march for Chihuahua was begun on the 14th by three hundred men, followed on the 16th and 18th by the rest of the regiment, and Lieutenant-Colonel Mitchell of Price's second regiment with ninety men.

This march in its beginning encountered the celebrated Jornada del Muerto of ninety miles, destitute of water and fuel. It is across a bend of the Rio Grande, and is cut off from that river by mountainous ground.

On Christmas day, at a spot called Bracito, when the regiment after its usual march, had picketed their horses, and were gathering fuel, the advance guard reported the rapid approach of the enemy in large force. Line was formed on foot, when a *black flag* was received with an insolent demand. Colonel Doniphan restrained his men from shooting the bearer down. The enemy's line, nearly half cavalry, and including a howitzer, opened fire at four hundred yards, and still advanced, and had fired three rounds, before fire was returned within effective range. Victory seems to have been decided by a charge of Captain Reid with twenty cavalry which he had managed to mount, and another charge by a dismounted company which captured the howitzer. The enemy fled, with loss of forty-three killed and one hundred and fifty wounded; our loss seven wounded, who all recovered.

The enemy were about twelve hundred strong; five hundred cavalry, the rest infantry, including several hundred El Paso militia; our force was five hundred—Lieutenant-Colonel Jackson with a part of the regiment arriving on the ground after the action. Colonel Doniphan gave credit "for the most essential service in forming the line and during the engagement" to Captain Thompson, First dragoons, "acting his aid and adviser."

December 27th.—He entered El Paso, and learning that General Wool was not in possession of Chihuahua, he sent to Santa Fè for one of the batteries of volunteer artillery; and waiting its arrival remained at El Paso until February 8th.

NEW MEXICO AND CALIFORNIA.

He then resumed his march for Chihuahua; with nine hundred and twenty-four effective men, and three hundred and fifteen heavy traders' wagons accompanied his march.

February 28th.—At the Pass of the Sacramento, fifteen miles from Chihuahua, the enemy was discovered in great force strongly posted, fortified by entrenchments, and well supplied with artillery. After an effective cannonade by the battery, Colonel Doniphan advanced to the attack, with seven companies dismounted in line, and three mounted. The decisive action of the battle was a charge by the two twelve-pound howitzers supported by three troops of cavalry, and followed up by the dismounted line and the rest of the artillery; the howitzers " unlimbered within fifty yards of the redoubts of the enemy," who were attacked by *sabre in their entrenchments.*

The enemy were finally put to flight with a loss of about six hundred men, and all their artillery, ten pieces; our strength was " nine hundred and forty effective men." Our loss nine killed and wounded.

Next day, March 1st, the army took formal possession of the capital of Chihuahua.

Colonel Doniphan had been ordered by General

Kearny to report to General Wool. At Chihuahua he provided for the safety of American citizens and their very large caravan property, and then determined to encounter all the risks of another great march; and, accordingly, with little or no loss, reached Monterey, where he reported to General Taylor.*

The Mormon battalion arrived at Santa Fè October 12th, and next day, Lieutenant Colonel Cooke assumed command. It had been commanded by Lieutenant A. J. Smith,† first dragoons, in its long march from Fort Leavenworth.

* I suspect that in this great venture they encountered, as a milder incident of war, most danger from the fire of the feminine eyes of the simple inhabitants; (but were they "ready" in their boasted "rags and roughness" for the courts of Venus?)

The advance on General Taylor's line of invasion had been wisely abandoned for a far shorter one to the heart and capital of Mexico; and the regiment was ordered home for discharge. It marched to Matamoras, carrying with them, nine hundred miles from Chihuahua, their ten captured cannon; there it embarked for New Orleans, St. Louis and Liberty, Missouri; making a grand circuit which counted miles by the thousand, and throwing a coloring of romantic adventure over the realities of its services; its share in the conquest of far-distant New Mexico—its pursuit of the Navajos beyond the snow-clad mountains of San Juan, and the pacification of that powerful tribe—its battles, and the great victory of Sacramento.

It received an ovation in Saint Louis, and a rejoicing welcome amid its homes in extreme western Missouri.—Not a fatted calf, but a half tamed buffalo cow, belonging to the author, was a contribution to a barbecue given for their entertainment.

† As Smith is not a very distinctive name, it may be interesting to mention that this one, now of Saint Louis, became a very distinguished Major General.

Every thing conspired to discourage the extraordinary undertaking of marching this battalion eleven hundred miles, for the much greater part through an unknown wilderness without road or trail, and with a wagon train.

It was enlisted too much by families; some were too old,—some feeble, and some too young; it was embarrassed by many women; it was undisciplined; it was much worn by travelling on foot, and marching from Nauvoo, Illinois; their clothing was very scant;—there was no money to pay them,—or clothing to issue; their mules were utterly broken down; the Quartermaster department was without funds, and its credit bad; and mules were scarce. Those procured were very inferior, and were deteriorating every hour for lack of forage or grazing. So every preparation must be pushed,—hurried. A small party with families, had been sent from Arkansas crossing up the river, to winter at a small settlement close to the mountains, called Pueblo. The battalion was now inspected, and eighty-six men found inefficient, were ordered, under two officers, with nearly all the women, to go to the same point; five wives of officers were reluctantly allowed to accompany the march, but furnished their own transportation.

By special arrangement and consent, the battalion was paid in checks,—not very available at Santa Fè.

With every effort the Quartermaster could only undertake to furnish rations for sixty days; and in fact full rations of only flour, sugar, coffee and salt; salt pork only for thirty days, and soap for twenty. To venture without pack saddles would be grossly imprudent, and so that burden was added.

October 19th the battalion was pushed out, by companies, six miles to Agua Frio; where some grazing might be had.

After dispatching a multitude of last duties, I left town and arrived in camp at sunset. Here I found all huddled in the sandy creek bottom; no grass; many mules without ropes or picket pins: they, and the beeves and oxen were to be herded under rather difficult circumstances. Some fodder had been procured.

The battalion have never been drilled, and, though obedient, have little discipline; they exhibit great heedlessness and ignorance, and some obstinacy.

I have brought road tools and have *determined* to take through my wagons; but the experiment is not a fair one, as the mules are nearly broken down at the outset. The only good ones, about twenty which I bought near Albuquerque, were taken for the express for Fremont's mail,—the General's order requiring "the twenty-one *best* in Santa Fè."

Next day a march of ten miles was made to the last water on the road to the river; an order of regulations for the march was issued; and the ration was lowered to twelve ounces of flour, and three-fourths allowance of sugar and coffee; but that of beef increased one-fifth,—to a pound and a half.

Extracts from Colonel Cooke's official journal will be given; some as specimens of daily doings; some of incidents or other matters of unusual interest,—à few of apparently insuperable obstacles and dangers, necessarily encountered, and overcome,— or endured.

"*October* 21st.—I ordered a very early reveille and march, to accomplish the twenty-four miles. I got the wagons ready before eight o'clock; having ordered, as a spur, that each company should send off its baggage as soon as ready; and that they should march in that order. At the last moment I learned that nineteen beeves and fourteen mules were missing. I had ordered that the guard—increased to twenty-seven privates—should guard the animals by night; a corporal and four privates, butchers, should drive the oxen; and a corporal,—on daily duty,—and six of the guard, drive and take care of the extra mules (except during the night). I had broken up yesterday, an old wagon I found here, for the axles, and the spokes, ordered to be made into picket pins. I was, of course, without mounted men to send after the missing cattle. I sent the officer of the day, and every member of the old guard in pursuit, in four parties, with orders to re-assemble here, and none to come on until all the animals were recovered; but this consumed an hour.

They were all recovered. I passed the whole column and reached the Gallisteo at eleven o'clock, and found it was possible to water there. I stopped until all had passed me, directing them to move on down, so that all the animals should be taken from the wagons, and should drink at the same time. I was on the ground an hour and three-quarters before the last wagon passed me. Each company marches in the rear of its baggage. On this terrible sandy road, down the stream, several oxen fell, and had to be rolled out of the road, they making no motion; the feet of others were bleeding. The last of the command have got into camp at nine P. M.,—several wagons not getting nearer than a mile. I had a little wood brought from the last hill top; there is none here. I had sent forward my interpreter, who only succeeded in buying twenty-four bushels of ears of corn. Lieutenant Smith, assistant-commissary of subsistence, and Lieutenant Stoneman, acting assistant quartermaster, arrived from Santa Fè since dark."

October 23d.—Next day eleven miles were accomplished, to San Bernalli. Many mules failed, and efforts to hire wagons failed, owing to the ill disposition of the citizens of property; and so again to-day. There was rain and wind last night, and I slept under a fallen tent. Many are sick. I determined to purchase mules, if possible. Passed the camp of a major and three companies of Price's regiment, who left Santa Fè, four days before the battalion; the major said, "after a day's march it took him two or three to collect the animals."

The assistant-quartermaster succeeded in exchanging thirty mules, worthless to us, for fifteen good ones, and also in purchasing ten. At Albuquerque I bought twelve fanegas of ears of corn, and crossed the river; making my way through three miles of very bad road. I encamped with comparatively good grass, and near the camp of Captain Burgwin (from General Kearny's column) where he had arrived this afternoon.

Here I purchased of officers eight mules with treasury drafts, and exchanged as many for better public animals, and also obtained twenty oxen. The captain also kindly exchanged two *ponton* wagons for very poor and heavy ones. This may be very important.

It rained again last night. This has been a day of hard and unremitting labor to me.

Next morning Captain Burgwin received a letter from the American traders below, stating General Armijo was marching up to seize their property, and asking protection. A pack of Indian goods, left for me by General Kearny was received from Captain Burgwin.

Mr. Stoneman was much disgusted to-day by the

contemptuous refusal of a nabob named Chavis, to sell or exchange mules.

I have ordered pork to be issued every fourth day. I also issued an order of further regulations. I assembled the captains this morning at reveille, and earnestly exhorted them to lend me more efficient assistance in requiring the mules to be properly grazed and fed; or else the expedition must soon fall through. They made excellent promises. I reduced to the ranks a first sergeant for failing to form the company at reveille, and giving the excuse that it was not light enough to call his roll. The mules are now turned loose and herded, while in camp.

"*October* 26*th*.—Marched at eight o'clock. Passed several villages. I sent across the river to Otero's store at Valencia, for some pack blankets, for which the assistant quartermaster had an order, and for purchase of mules. Otero, like Chavis—both malcontents—asked unreasonable prices. He had lost, yesterday evening, five or six thousand sheep; two shepherds killed by the Indians. He had been riding all night hiring men to pursue them.

I stopped some time in a settlement of the Luna

family. All the effective males had gone after the Navajos, who had also stolen six thousand six hundred sheep of them yesterday; and as they say, killed two of their shepherds. I wrote for Señora Luna a note to Captain Burgwin. She thought herself and the other women dangerously exposed. But what can Burgwin do with broken down mules, all the best having been selected by General Kearny? I am still sick of a cold; they are very prevalent. We are exposed to black frost nightly, without fuel. The mules are getting sore shoulders. I called up the captains and gave them a lecture on the subject, as to fitting and cleaning collars, shortening harness, etc. and relieving mules, about to become galled; for I have assigned all the mules, giving two extra ones for every team; the march thirteen miles. Saw mother and daughter to-day,—the latter thirteen and married,—as usual here, at that age; both fine looking, with the large liquid eyes of the Señora."

Two days of similar progress, to camp near Sabinal. Rainy and very cold weather, the mountains opposite covered with snow; "scarcely a large *weed* within a mile or two of camp." The roads very heavy from sand.

October 29*th.*—Marched ten miles to the bottom below La Joya,—where I found my two dragoons, mules and property all safe. Sent Lieutenant Smith to go in advance and purchase three hundred sheep which, with the beeves, will make sixty days' rations from Santa Fè. I have extreme difficulty in having the mules properly cared for; there is great *vis inertiæ* in such a command.

Next day, a sand hill reaching the river bank was encountered; two hours, with teams doubled, and twenty men to a wagon, were required to reach its top,—only three or four hundred paces. Reaching Pulvidera, to get grass it was necessary to pass a very large canal; the men worked well with spades and large hoes, furnished by some Mexicans, who worked with them unasked; but it was a difficult job; and a wagon hound was broken.

November 2*d.*—The battalion has marched twenty seven miles in the last two days; the valley continues much narrowed,—with variegated scenery and woods. Many oxen broke down; and wagons were sent back empty with teams little better.

General Armijo it was learned had been sent South under guard, and wrote to his wife to lend money freely to our army; and that the enemy were gathering volunteers at El Paso. Captain Burgwin, going to the protection of the caravans, was encamped two miles from the battalion.

The three hundred sheep were brought into camp, but proved to be very poor,—mostly lambs; also the required beeves, very poor. The guides engaged by General Kearny arrived, with very discouraging accounts, and said it was at least ninety days' travel to the Pacific. They were sent forward to decide where to leave the Rio Grande, and make some explorations beyond, returning to meet the battalion there.

"All the vexations and troubles of any other three days of my life have not equalled those of the last twenty-four hours. . . . My attention is constantly on the stretch for the smallest things. I have to order, and then see that it is done."

This day the road we have followed, passed to the east of the river; it being the head of the Jernada del Muerto; the river sweeping off to the south-west in a great bend. Consequently the battalion continued on General Kearny's trail.

On Captain Burgwin's march, near Luna village,

some inhabitants met him at speed, reporting the Navajos had just robbed them, and taken off a woman (as I apprehended, when I wrote to him). Captain Greer's company, which was much in advance, was sent instantly to the rescue, half his men a-foot. He overtook and re-captured the cattle and sheep, and following on about sixteen miles, the mules of his company exhausted and left, and his men following with long intervals on foot, the Captain, Lieutenant Wilson, Corporal Price and one private (on horses got of the Mexicans), overtook four Navajos; then uprose from a ravine fifty others, who surrounded the captain and party. These last killed two Indians outright, and then retreated in good order under a shower of arrows, and were pursued, in their turn, a quarter of a mile, until they fell upon a few of their footmen, and thus came off unwounded.

My camp is in an open grove of the river bottom. We rejoice for once in plenty of fuel and good fires. In every direction are lofty mountains, blue from distance or haze, and capped with snow fields.

In this bottom I saw a flock of many thousand

sheep, probably the last. I sent Lieutenant Smith with $100 to purchase eighty, to make up for the lambs. I ordered him to give the same price as yesterday, and to *take them*. He got them. I shall use about ten of the oxen for beef. I have hired three Mexicans and put the three hundred and eighty sheep under their exclusive charge. I found that we could improve on the track made by the dragoons.

November 3d.—The camp was visited this morning by Captain Grier and one of our merchants. Reports of the war had been received by way of Chihuahua; "the Americans were in Monterey, but invested by superior force of Mexicans," etc.

There have been strong suspicions down here, of a conspiracy to rise and throw off the American rule in this territory; connected perhaps at the moment, with the advance of seven hundred men who certainly did march from El Paso north; and there is no doubt they have emissaries above. I learn the last express to Captain Burgwin brought news of a talk in Santa Fè of a rising of the people. As for myself I believe that the priests and some of the millionaires would like to put forward others to attempt to regain their despotic sway and grinding oppression of the people; but take them all together I think the cowardly barbarians,—too fortunate in having a decent government forced upon them,—are selfish enough to refrain from any risk in the world.

I marched to-day fourteen miles; some bad bluffs of heavy sand were passed. .The camp is on a high plain, covered with grama grass, apparently quite dead, but *said* to be nearly as good as grain. For the last forty miles the flat river bottom is perhaps two miles in width, some of it richer than above. There is however, a white efflorescence, rather more frequent here than there, which is said to contain carbonate of potash, and to render the soil unfit for agriculture. This district, entirely unoccupied, has the great advantage over that above, so thickly inhabited, of forests covering perhaps one-fourth of the bottoms, and the mountains also covered with cedar very near. Fear of the Indians has kept it a desert.

We have severe frosts at night, and hot days. I have reduced the ration to nine ounces of flour, and ten of pork.

I met one of the guides, whom Leroux, their chief, sent back, ostensibly to settle upon smoke signals, but really, I suspect because he was of no use. The fellow weighs two hundred pounds, and has been drinking for a week or two; I ordered his discharge.

It took a cow and twelve of the lambs to make out the ration to-night. Dr. Foster, the interpreter, calls a large bush, found here, the mezquit; there is a growth common on the Missouri and Platte prairies, much smaller and more delicate, which I am sure is the same, or nearly allied. I could never hear of a name for it there, although I think old Captain Boone used to call it bastard locust.

The cactus here is ten feet high.

November 9th.—In six days, resting one, the battalion could only make forty miles, in about the same number of hours' work, camping this day at the point where General Kearny struck out from the river toward the copper mines.

This slow progress was over very bad ground, without a road;—deep sand, steep hills and rocks, ten miles together, without river-bottom land; the men, nearly all of them, laboring in aid of the weak teams to move the wagons.

The country had changed its character and was now rough, surrounded by mountains and characterized by grama grass, cedars, mezquite and other strange growths. Game made its appearance: bears, deer, and beavers; some of these last were trapped by Charboneaux, an active half-breed guide. The weather grew warmer, but with one rain and wind storm.

Mr. Leroux returned; he had left the river where it turned eastward opposite San Diego, and had found a water hole fifteen miles on our course, and seen a prairie stream about thirty miles beyond.

"It has now become evident that we cannot go on so, with any prospect of a successful or safe termination to the expedition. The guides say that most of the mules could not be driven loose to California. I have carefully examined them and found that whole teams seem ready to break down. The three remaining ox teams were to go back about this time, at the latest; twenty-two men are on the sick report; quite a number have been transported in the wagons, and the knapsacks and arms of others; there are still in the battalion men old, weakly, and trifling; besides all this, the rations are insufficient.

I have determined and ordered that fifty-five of the sick and least efficient men shall return to Santa Fè; that they shall take rations for twenty-six days, —but of flour only ten ounces to the ration, and of pork, eight. I shall thus be relieved of one thousand eight hundred pounds weight of rations, and by means of what they leave of the rations provided for them, particularly the live stock, make an important increase of rations for the remainder. But I have also determined to send back, if possible, only one team of oxen, and use for my mule wagons the ten other yokes (the other wagons can be sent for;— Captain Burgwin is only fifty-eight miles above). There are some thirty loose mules which some think will do nearly as well if packed only sixty or eighty pounds. I have ordered the upright tent poles to be left, muskets to be used as substitutes; and tents to be reduced to one for nine men (which they will hold, if opened and lowered to the height of a musket). This all carried out, I trust with perseverance and energy to accomplish the undertaking;

though in a few days I commence a route of over three hundred miles—to the San Pedro River—of which the guides know little or nothing; Leroux thinking himself very fortunate in finding water at an interval of thirty miles at the outset. The whole route is now said to be three hundred miles longer than was believed when at Santa Fè; and ten miles, making the road as we go, is a hard day's work—equal to twenty miles or more of a good road."

In that camp an express was received from Captain Burgwin, reporting information that a large party of the enemy were coming from the South by the copper-mine route.

The return party, under a subaltern, was got off on the 10th; but it consumed the day. A large number of tents, poles, camp kettles, and mess pans were put in a wagon to be left under charge of a beaver trapping party found there; the saddles and packs were prepared, and some tried on, under the instruction of the guides and other Mexicans. Leroux, with several assistant guides, was ordered to depart early next day to make further exploration, and to send back one or two guides from a new point, to meet the battalion at the last water then known, while he shall explore still further on.

About twenty-nine miles were made in the next two days, with improvement of ground, chiefly in river bottom, which had increased to a mile in width, with a wide strip of timber; the country to the west gradually flattening; mountains rising abruptly from the eastern bank; but an apparently complete gap was observed, which was thought to be where the "jornada" road approaches within four or five miles of the river; if so, it is where a future road should cross and fall into the one now being made.

There was an evident improvement of means; thirty-six mules were lightly packed, besides oxen; some of which " performed antics that were irresistibly ludicrous, (owing to the crupper perhaps,) such as jumping high from the ground, many times in quick-step time, turning round the while,—a perfect jig."

"On the 11th, while Charboneaux was making a rather remote exploration for water, I rode a mile through willows, weeds and reeds above my head, and found some in a densely timbered and brushy bottom, and established the camp on the bluff, with fine grass near. The tents are pitched with muskets somewhat lengthened by a peg that enters the muzzle; the backs are opened and a gore inserted, so that they are stretched out into nearly a circle, and are very capacious.

The 12th was a fortunate day; the pioneers were several times at bad spots just ready for the wagons as they arrived; and I discovered just in time to set the wagons right, that we had got into a *cul de sac*. I had calculated that the wagons would be lightened above twenty per cent, while the rations were increased eight days. This is confirmed by the facility of motion.

November 13*th*.—A mile or two from camp a note from Leroux was found on a pole, but also two return guides were met, who directed the march short to the right; and a march of fifteen miles was made in a south-west course, always ascending over gravelly prairie, uneven but not very difficult; and then, in a rocky chasm a hundred feet deep, a natural well or reservoir of pure water was found. There was no fuel, save a few bushes and Spanish bayonet, but the country was well covered with grama and buffalo grass.

And here, before describing this unique venture of the exploration by a battalion with a wagon train, of the unknown wilderness which must be passed to reach California, it will serve the unities of place, and nearly of time, to pause, and to record the completion of the conquest of New Mexico. For there soon occurred an uprising against our bloodless, but perhaps stern change of rule, which had found temporary success, chiefly, it is believed, through an audacious surprise. And it proved that the best traits of our nature at a low stage, combine with the forces of ignorance and confirmed customs and habits, to resent and resist an abrupt and forcible bestowal of the greatest boons—the comforts of civilization—Liberty itself!

II.

THE INSURRECTION IN NEW MEXICO AND THE FINAL CONQUEST.

ABOUT the middle of December, Colonel Price, Second Missouri Mounted Volunteers, left in command by Colonel Doniphan, received information that efforts to excite a general revolt were being made. A former officer of the Mexican army was arrested, and a list of all the disbanded Mexican soldiers was found on his person. Then many others, supposed to be implicated, were arrested; but the two leaders, Ortiz and Archuleta, made their escape to the South. A full investigation revealed that many of the most influential persons in the northern part of the territory were engaged in the conspiracy. But these prompt measures seemed to be effectual in preventing an insurrection.

Charles Bent, the Governor, appointed by General Kearny, was an able man; amiable, and married to a native of the country, he was considered quite popular; January 14th he left Santa Fè to visit his family at San Fernando de Taos,—near the Pueblo de Taos, about seventy miles north of Santa Fè, and near the top of the great southern promontory of the Rocky Mountains. There, January 19th, the governor, the sheriff, the circuit attorney, the prefect and two others, were "murdered in the most inhuman manner that savages could devise." The same day seven Americans were also murdered at Arroyo Hondo, and two others on the Rio Colorado. The prefect, Vigil, was a New Mexican; and the intention was apparent to murder every one who had accepted office under American rule.

Colonel Price received this startling news at Santa Fè the next day, and at the same time intercepted letters calling upon the people of the lower river for aid; he heard also of the approach, from the north, of a constantly swelling force of insurgents.

The Colonel immediately dispatched orders to Albuquerque, to Major Edmonson, to march up and occupy Santa Fè; and to Captain Burgwin of the first dragoons, to march north, with one of his troops to join him in the field. The Colonel marched,

January 23d, at the head of only three hundred and fifty men, to meet the rebels; this force was all infantry or dismounted cavalry, except a troop which volunteered in Santa Fè under Felix St. Vrain, and also four twelve pound mountain howitzers. It included Captain Angney's little battalion, which so gallantly contended with the cavalry for the lead in the invasion of the Territory.

Next day Captain St. Vrain, in advance, encountered the enemy on heights commanding the road, near the town of Cañada, and also occupying some strong adobe houses at the base of the hills. Price formed line, and advanced the howitzers, which opened fire. A detachment of the enemy made a movement to cut off our baggage train, then more than a mile to the rear; the manœuvre being observed, Captain St. Vrain was sent to counteract it, and succeeded in bringing up the train.

After a sharp cannonade, Price ordered Angney's battalion to assault the nearest houses, from which issued a galling fire on his right flank; the houses were handsomely carried; a general charge was then made; the artillery and three companies assaulted successfully several houses in a grove from which a sharp fire had been kept up; and St. Vrain commenced a movement to gain the enemy's rear. In a short time the enemy were in full flight, and Cañada was occupied.

Our loss was two men killed, and a lieutenant and six men wounded. The insurgents, estimated at fifteen hundred in number, left thirty-six killed.

Next morning the New Mexicans showed in some force on the distant heights, but on the approach of a detachment, sent to attack them, soon disappeared.

Colonel Price advanced up the Rio del Norte as far as Luceros, and early on the 28th, was joined there by Captain Burgwin,—who brought his dismounted company by forced marches,—by an additional company of his own regiment, mounted, and also by Lieut. Wilson, First Dragoons, with a six pounder, which had been sent for.

On the 29th, with about four hundred and eighty rank and file, Colonel Price advanced to La Joya, and there learned that a party of the enemy occupied a very strong pass or cañon, leading to Embudo, but on a country road that was impracticable for artillery and wagons; he therefore detached

Captain Burgwin with three companies, including St. Vrain's, to attack them and force a passage. Capt. Burgwin found the enemy six or seven hundred strong, on the sides of the mountains at the narrowest part of the gorge; they were protected by dense masses of cedar trees, and large fragments of rock. He dismounted St. Vrain's company, and sent it to attack the slopes on the left, and a second company those to the right. Both companies advanced rapidly in open order, firing with much execution, and the enemy soon fled with a speed that defied all pursuit. Capt. Burgwin marched through the defile into the open valley, and then occupied Embudo without opposition. Our loss was one killed and one severely wounded; both of St. Vrain's company. The insurgents' loss was reported twenty killed and sixty wounded.

On the 30th, Burgwin marched to Trampas, where he was joined next day by Price, when the whole force marched to Chamisola.

February 1st, the summit of the mountain was reached, and the next day the command quartered in the small village of Rio Chiquito, at the entrance to the valley of Taos. These two marches were through snow so deep that the troops had to break the track for the artillery and wagons; many of the men were frost bitten.

February 3d, Price marched through Fernando de Taos to the Pueblo, which he found strongly fortified. It was enclosed by formidable walls and strong pickets; within the enclosure and near the northern and southern walls were two large buildings of irregular pyramidal form, seven or eight stories in height, each capable of sheltering five or six hundred men. Besides these and similar smaller buildings, a large church was situated in the northwest angle, with a narrow passage between it and the outer wall. The exterior walls and all the enclosed buildings were pierced for rifles; every point of the exterior walls was flanked by projecting buildings.

The western flank of the church was selected for attack, and at 2 P. M., Lieut. Dyer, of the Ordnance Department, opened fire from the battery at about two hundred and fifty yards. The fire by the six pounder, and howitzers was kept up about two hours, when, as the ammunition wagon had not come up, and the troops were suffering from cold and fatigue, the forces were withdrawn to San Fernando.

Colonel Price reported—" Early on the morning of the fourth, I again advanced upon Pueblo. Posting the dragoons under Captain Burgwin about two hundred and sixty yards from the western flank of the church, I ordered the mounted men under Captains St. Vrain and Slack, to a position on the opposite side of the town, whence they could discover and intercept any fugitive who might attempt to escape towards the mountains, or in the direction of San Fernando. The residue of the troops took ground about three hundred yards from the northern wall. Here, too, Lieut. Dyer established himself with the six pounder and two howitzers, while Lt. Hassendaubel, of Major Clark's battalion light artillery, remained with Captain Burgwin, in command of two howitzers. By this arrangement a cross-fire was obtained, sweeping the front and eastern flank of the church.

"All these arrangements being made, the batteries opened upon the town at nine o'clock A. M. At eleven o'clock, finding it impossible to breach the walls of the church with the six pounder and howitzers, I determined to storm the building. At a signal, Captain Burgwin, at the head of his own company, and that of Captain McMillin, charged the western flank of the church, while Captain Angney, infantry battalion, and Captain Barber and Lieutenant Boon, Second Mo. Mounted Volunteers, charged the northern wall. As soon as the troops above mentioned, had established themselves under the western wall of the church, axes were used in the attempt to breach it; and a temporary ladder having been made, the roof was fired. About this time Captain Burgwin, at the head of a small party, left the cover afforded by the flank of the church, and penetrating into the corral in front of that building, endeavored to force the door. In this exposed situation, Captain Burgwin received a severe wound, which deprived me of his valuable services, and of which he died on the 7th instant. Lieutenants McIlvaine, First U. S. Dragoons, and Royall and Lackland, Second Regiment Volunteers, accompanied Captain Burgwin into the corral; but the attempt on the church door proved fruitless, and they were compelled to retire behind the wall. In the mean time small holes had been cut in the western wall, and shells were thrown in by hand, doing good execution. The six pounder was now brought around by Lieutenant Wilson, who at the distance of two hundred yards, poured a heavy fire of grape into the town. The enemy during all of this time kept up a destructive fire upon our troops. About half past three o'clock, the six pounder was run up within sixty yards of the church, and after ten rounds, one of the holes which had been cut with the axes was widened into a practicable breach. The storming party, among whom were Lieutenant Dyer of the ordnance, and Lieutenants Wilson and Taylor, First dragoons, entered and took possession of the church, without opposition. The interior was filled with dense smoke, but for which circumstance our storming party would have suffered great loss. A few of the enemy were seen in the gallery, where an open door admitted the air, but they retired without firing a gun. The troops left to support the battery on the north, were now ordered to charge on that side. The enemy abandoned the western part of the town. Many took refuge in the large houses on the east, while others endeavored to escape toward the mountains. These latter were pursued by the mounted men under Captain Slack and St. Vrain, who killed fifty-one of them, only two or three men escaping. It was now night, and our troops were quietly quartered in the houses which the enemy had abandoned. On the next morning the enemy sued for peace, and thinking the severe loss they had sustained would prove a salutary lesson, I granted their supplication, on the condition that they should deliver up to me Tomas, —one of their principal men, who had instigated and been actively engaged in the murder of Governor Bent and others. The number of the enemy at the battle of Pueblo de Taos was between six and seven hundred. Of these about one hundred and fifty were killed—wounded not known. Our own loss was seven killed and forty-five wounded; many of the wounded have since died.

"The principal leaders in this insurrection were Tafoya, Pablo Chavis, Pablo Montoya, Cortez and Tomas, a Pueblo Indian. Of these, Tafoya was killed at Cañada; Chavis was killed at Pueblo; Montoya was hanged at Don Fernando on the 7th instant, and Tomas was shot by a private while in the guard room at the latter town. Cortez is still at large.

This person was at the head of rebels in the valley of the Mora."

Thus in the prime of life, James H. K. Burgwin of North Carolina, captain in First Regiment of Dragoons, fell in the brave performance of duty. He was accomplished, amiable, and much beloved.

It was lamentable that the Pueblos should in this single case, have been induced by some strong deceptions and incitements, to take up arms. The above full account of their remarkable aboriginal progress in the defensive art of war, through which they resisted for two days an artillery siege, and the singular defensive form of their dwelling houses, which as citadels saved the most of their lives in the assault, is given as most interesting. In the heat of the assault, a dragoon was in the act of killing a woman, unrecognized by dress, similar to the man's, and both sexes wearing the hair long; in this extremity she saved her life by an act of the most conclusive personal exposure! Seven years after, the author raised, in half a day, a company of irregulars in this same town, to serve against the Apaches, and efficient fine fellows they were.

The insurrection was general in the northern and

eastern part of the territory. Vegas was saved from revolt by the presence of a garrison; near there, and other northern posts of troops, were rather distant grazing camps; they were attacked with some execution, and the loss of the animals. Some public and sutler trains were robbed of all their oxen and mules. At the handsome village of Mora, eighteen miles west of the present Fort Union, eight Americans were murdered. January 22d, Capt. Hendley, Second Missouri Volunteers, marched there from Vegas the 24th, with eighty men; he found it occupied by above one hundred and fifty men; he engaged with a number, attempting to enter the town, who were supported by a sally; he then assaulted the town; he penetrated from house to house, some of which were destroyed, and into one end of their fort, where he was killed and several were wounded. Lieut. McKarney then—apprehending the return of from three hundred to five hundred men, who had left there that day for Pueblo—withdrew, and marched back to Las Vegas, with fifteen prisoners; he reported fifteen to twenty of the enemy slain.

January 30th, the camp of Capt. Robinson was surprised, and two hundred horses and mules driven off, and one man killed and two wounded. Major Edmonson marched to his relief from Vegas, and afterward followed the banditti into a dangerous cañon of the Canadian River at the mouth of the Mora; he reported, " the hills around them literally covered with Indians and Mexicans," estimated to be above four hundred. He fought his way through with much difficulty; but having to return the next day through the same cañon, he found " that the enemy had left on the night after the battle in great haste, leaving horses, cattle, camp equipage, etc., not taking time to scalp or strip our men lost in the action, as is their custom." He pursued, but found that they had dispersed after dividing their spoil. The enemy's loss was reported to be forty-one killed.

June 27th, Lieut. R. T. Brown, Second Missouri Volunteers, went with two volunteers and a Mexican guide in pursuit of some horses which had been driven off from Vegas; he found them at Las Vallas, fifteen miles south, and attempting to seize them, the Mexicans resisted, and attacked and killed the whole party. Major Edmonson then marched from Vegas, surprised the town, shot down a few who attempted to escape, took forty prisoners and sent them to Sante Fè for trial.

On the sixth of July, the grazing camp of Captain Morris's company was attacked; Lieutenant Larkin and four men were killed, and nine wounded, and all the horses and other property fell into the hands of the outlaws. Lieutenant-Colonel Willock marched from Taos in their pursuit, but could not overtake them.

Colonel Price reported July 20th that his command was so reduced by the departure of companies whose time had expired, that he considered it necessary to concentrate all his forces at Santa Fè; that rumors of insurrection were rife, and also of a large force approaching from the South; he adds, "it is certain that the New Mexicans entertain deadly hatred against the Americans."

His call for reinforcements had been anticipated; and by autumn, fresh volunteer regiments from Missouri, engaged for the war, had swelled the force in New Mexico to above three thousand; about double the numbers of those who made the first audacious invasion, and apparent conquest.

And New Mexico then submitted.

III.

THE INFANTRY MARCH TO THE PACIFIC.

THE Mormon battalion was left fifteen miles west of the Rio Grande, in camp near a deep ravine in which was a natural well of rock, which the sagacity of the guides had discovered, to make their first venture in the desert a success. This was November the 13th, 1846.

Next day it entered upon a grassy plain extending indefinitely to the south-west; small isolated mountains rose here and there to view, but a low range barred the better course westward; four miles out, a guide was met, reporting Leroux and the others at a mountain streamlet eight miles off, and more to the north. The camp was made there.

"Thus Leroux, on his second trip—or third, if he attempted the exploration promised by the General, —has only reached about forty miles from the river! I have no guide that knows any thing about the country; and I fear such exploring will prove slow and hazardous work. He goes to-morrow with six men, and is to send back one for each of my marches. The weather is cold and boisterous, threatening snow. We find here apparently the remains of a stone house, but only a foot or two high, showing no marks of tools; also many fragments of pottery, and a broken mortar of very hard red stone, etc."

The 15th, it blew a gale with rain, snow, and sunshine, alternately; as there was fuel, and the guides were behind hand, the battalion did not move.

Next day it marched to the south, skirting the foot of the mountain about thirteen miles, and camped at a small swampy hole of water near a gap of the mountain. (This has found its way to some of the maps as Cooke's Spring.) There was no wood, but brush answered for fuel. " Charboneaux has returned, and reports the gap in front of us to be practicable, and that there is water six miles on; he went with the others about twelve miles beyond it, without finding other water."

On the 17th, the gap was passed without much

difficulty, and turning north, the water was found up a ravine to the right, but only three miles from the other camp. As the guide had gone twelve miles further without discovering water, it was necessary to camp there.

"I saw to-day a new variety of oak, a large luxuriant bush, eight or ten feet high, with leaves about an inch long; they are still very green: * also a new and very beautiful variety of the Spanish bayonet: very large and spherical in shape, the largest leaves (or spikes) three feet long, and indented like a fine saw, with a stalk eighteen feet high from the centre. Tasson, a guide, hunted and killed in the mountain, two goats which were found to have cropped ears.

"At this camp the California partridge was first observed. They are rounder, smoother, and have longer necks than ours, with a beautiful plume to the head, and are slate colored. Also a cactus of hemispherical form, fifteen to eighteen inches in diameter, with ridges armed with horny hooks three inches long. Thirty mortar holes cut into flat rocks were found this morning."

* Since named Quercus emoryi.

November 18*th.*—The battalion marched eighteen miles in a north-west course to the Mimbres, (osiers, some of which were there found,) a clear, bold stream, running to the south, but sinking a little below the camp.

Next day in a south-west course, slightly ascending over a smooth prairie, to Ojo de Vaca, (Cow Spring) about eighteen miles were made. This spring is on a road from the copper mines to Yanos.

November 20th, spent in camp, was an anxious day. The guides had all returned, having found a little water in the end of a ridge, in a south-west course toward San Bernadino—a deserted rancho, known only by report. They had gone only about twelve miles further in that direction, but the absence of any indication of water, had discouraged and turned them back. By common consent the certainty of water at that point (thought to be about seventy, but really above one hundred miles distant) made it an objective point; for all shrink instinctively from entering the vast table land to the west, where no broken ground, no hill, no tree, could be seen from a stand-point four hundred feet high. The despairing wanderer whose life depends upon finding water, always turns with hope to a mountain, to a tree, or to broken ground.¹

A high peak, close to the spring, was ascended, and anxious consultation there held. ⌈This road, for copper ore, led to Yanos; my interpreter had been there the previous summer; he and the guides were positive it lay to the south-west, six or seven days' marches; the interpreter knew there was a road or trail from there to the presidios Fronteras and Tucson due west.⌋ This would surely be giving up the discovery of "a wagon road to the Pacific!" The staff officers and the captains were taken into council; they, the guides and Mr. Hall, (the volunteer and M. C. elect, who had accompanied their last exploration,) all agreed it was too great a risk to do otherwise than take this Yanos road.

It was found advisable at this camp, to order the issues of flour and fresh meat to be increased to ten and twenty-eight ounces.

November 21*st.*—I marched this morning by the road, of which the guides had pointed out the course, west of south. But I soon found it leaving level prairie in its first course, and leading over a ridge, twenty-five degrees east of south. I had relied on

6*

the assertions that Yanos was to the south-west, and balanced in my judgment of many other weighty considerations, had taken advice. I had followed the guides in almost every direction but eastward. After proceeding a mile and a half, without any further consultation, I turned short to the right, and directed the march to the hole of water which had been discovered to the south-west. . . I encamped there, at the foot of the ridge, the water being two miles up a narrow valley right away from my course. Whilst camping, fortunately, some water, enough for men's use, was found a quarter of a mile off.

Next day the battalion took a south-west course, preceded but two hours by the guides; the ground smooth, slightly descending, well covered with grass. To divide the greater labor of breaking the track, the leading company and its wagons, after an hour, were stopped until all had passed, and so with each in turn; this became the rule.

A signal smoke was seen in the afternoon—which should announce the discovery of water—perhaps fifteen miles off in front. Keeping its direction, camp was made at dusk, without water.

"Since dark Charboneaux has come in; his mule gave out, he says, and he stopped for it to rest and feed a half an hour; when going to saddle it, it kicked at him and ran off; he followed it a number of miles and finally shot it; partly I suppose from anger, and partly, as he says, to get his saddle and pistols, which he brought into camp."

Next morning the march began before sunrise. "All admired the singular and unusual beauty which followed its rising; but once or twice before had a mirage (caused on great plains by unusual vapor) been observed. A distant mountain ridge became the shore of a luminous lake, in which nearer mountains or hills showed as a vast city,—castles, churches, spires! even masts and sails of shipping could be seen by some."

In the mountain ridge the water was found, but it was not enough for the men to drink; it was soon gone, and the poor fellows were waiting for it to leak from the rocks, and dipping it with spoons! There was nothing to do but toil on over the ridge. Six miles beyond, a guide was met with news of water three leagues further on.

We came in sight of what was apparently a river,

but we believed it to be sand. For hours I rode on, approaching it obliquely, but seemed to get no nearer. At last I struck it after sundown, and found it something extraordinary; it was said to be the bottom of a long dry lake or swamp. It appeared, in the obscurity, something between smooth marble and a great sheet of ice; wagons moved with traces unstretched, and made no track. I sent to order those in the rear to bear to the right, and take advantage of it much sooner. I passed it in two miles, and found at its shore a swampy spot, with deep water holes.

The wagons arrived about eight o'clock, having been thirteen hours in motion. We had marched forty miles in thirty-six hours, without water. But for the dry lake, we should not have reached the water until the next day. Mr. Hall came to the right of the ridge, and he thought it a shorter way.

A small trading party of Mexicans was found at this point, where the battalion remained the next day, the two last wagons only coming up that night.

Twenty-one mules were purchased of the Mexicans, who gave a good report of a route to San Bernadino; and one of them was engaged as a guide, and to assist in opening communication with the

Apaches, whom they report to have plenty of mules, they having lately returned from a successful raid into Sonora.

The clay flat which is thirty miles long, is called by the Mexicáns Las Playas. "There occurred here, ten years ago, a very extraordinary and treacherous massacre. An American named Johnson with seventeen men of various nationalities, (with also a Mexican captain and four soldiers, but who are said to have left him before the occurrence) had come from Sonora on a plundering expedition against the Apaches, and for their scalps, for which fifty dollars each were then offered by the government of Sonora. Johnson met here above a hundred men, besides women and children of the Apaches, for trade; they had gathered round close, and unsuspected he had concealed a swivel between two bags of flour; it was loaded to the muzzle with balls and chain. A man sat smoking, and at the signal, uncovered the breech and fired; this was followed by two rapid discharges of small arms.

"At this explosion, seemingly from the ground, and unexpected as an earthquake, the Indians not mangled or killed, fled in consternation. Johnson's party soon retired and were followed and fired upon without effect by a party of the Apaches; but they killed seven more of them, and reached Yanos in rapid retreat. They took from the body of the chief, Juan José, who was slain, an order which Santa Anna in his Texan campaign, had sent to a general officer; the Indians had captured it. Johnson still lives in Sonora."

In the three days following, about forty miles were marched in the general south-west course, passing a low mountain gap, through broken country, finding some small streams and good grass.

"Whilst the train was crawling up the pass, I discovered Charboneaux near the summit in pursuit of bears. I saw three of them up among the rocks, whilst the bold hunter was gradually nearing them. Soon he fired, and in ten seconds again; then there was confused action, one bear falling down, the others rushing about with loud fierce cries, amid which the hunter's too, could be distinguished; the mountain fairly echoed. I much feared he was lost, but soon, in his red shirt, he appeared on a rock; he had cried out, in Spanish, for more balls. The bear was rolled down, and butchered before the wagons passed. It is a fact that both shots—and the ball of the second, passed from the hunter's mouth into the muzzle of his gun with only its weight to send it home—made but one hole in the bear's skin, in the side, and one ball ranged forward, the other back. . . . There is much that is strange on this table-land, studded with peaks and mountains of every shape; but this afternoon all must have been struck with the quiet beauty of the scene. The mountain passed, before us we saw a smooth plain, narrow, but unbounded to the front; the grama grass waving with the south wind, received from the slant sunshine a golden sheen; but the whole had a blue and purple setting of mountain ranges on either side; the light, the shadows, the varying distances gave variety and beauty of hue; the near heights dotted with cedars, the silvered granite peaks, and the far off summits of the Gila Mountains; and then the tree tops of the Las Animas, which we approached, gave the cheering promise, which the bracing air welcomed, of comfort and rest."

November 28th, a faint road was struck, believed to be from Yanos; it very soon led to a very precipitous and rocky descent of perhaps a thousand feet into the heart of a wild confusion of mountains, which extended as far as could be seen. It was soon discovered that the trail could not, at its first descent, at least, be made passable for the wagons; water within a mile was fortunately discovered, and the battalion camped. Leroux and all but one of the guides were still absent. Some exploration was then made; all pronounced the first descent impassable for wagons; but immediately a large party was sent to work a passage-way. That night Leroux arrived, bringing an Apache chief, whom he had managed with difficulty and much address. Next morning it was owing to Leroux's positive assertions and arguments, that there could be, and was no other pass but the horse trail, that I did not insist upon his thorough examination. He even asserted, but was mistaken, that he *had* examined an opening I had seen from an eminence, and believed might be a wagon road. Meanwhile the party continued, the second day, hard at work with crowbar, pick, etc., while I sent one company and about half the baggage, packed on mules, to the first water on the trail in a deep ravine below. It was about six miles, and the mules were brought back in the evening. Next morning they took the rest of the loading, and I succeeded that day with much labor and difficulty, in getting the wagons to the new camp. Some were let down by ropes, and one was broken. About this time, Doctor Foster, interpreter, accidentally found the intersection of an old wagon road with mine, and said he followed it back, and that it led to the verge of the plain about a mile from our point of descent. He says this is called the pass of Guadalope, and that it is the only one for many hundred miles to the south, by which the broken descent from the great table-land of Mexico can be made by wagons, and rarely by pack mules

" The scenery to-day was grand and picturesque. At one place there is a pass not thirty paces wide; on one side a cliff overhangs the road; just opposite on a vertical base of solid rock, forty feet high, rests another rock of a rounded cubical form of about twenty-five feet dimensions; on its top rests still another of spherical shape, twelve or fifteen feet in diameter. The mountains and sharp ravines were well covered with the new species of oak of large size, cedar, sycamore, etc., Spanish bayonet, mezquit and other shrubs, all of a bright green. We descended about one thousand feet. Private Allen has disappeared."

December 1st.—Seven miles were made down the dry bed of a mountain stream, and the pioneers went to the edge of a prairie, and returned. The scenery was beautiful; broken mountains, precipices, and a confusion of rocks; the mezcal and Spanish bayonet become trees; evergreen oaks, cottonwoods and sycamores brilliantly colored by frost. " Messrs. Smith, Hall, and myself have ascended a peak, near by, some eight hundred feet high. Our view was extensive. A few miles to the south, we saw the Huaqui, which becoming a large river, empties far down into the Gulf of California. To the north-west we saw a prairie for thirty or forty miles, narrowed by the mountains, seen every where else, to a gap-like outlet. We supposed that must be our course. San Bernadino was not visible. The top of the mountain was about thirty yards by fifteen. I suggested what a world's wonder it would be, set like a gem in the grounds of the capitol. The rocks, like all on this mountain, glittered with crystals of silex, white, pink, and even purple ; there grew a giant mezcal thirty feet high, and others of this year; bristling spheres of green bayonets, three feet long; several shrubs without a name; cacti, from a little pink ball at your feet, to the size of trees; a nondescript, thought to be of that family, sending out rods fourteen feet long, with rosin for bark, and two inch spikes for leaves, which I named 'devil rod,' etc."

That night thick ice formed in the tents. Next day the battalion was soon clear of the cañon, and eight miles brought them into and across wide meadows to the old houses of the rancho of San Bernadino; it is enclosed by a wall with two regular bastions; the spring is fifteen paces in diameter. The soil was thought good, but the grass at that time was poor; the rising ground beyond was a mezquit chaparral.

Before this rancho was desolated by the Apaches, there were reported to be eighty thousand cattle on it; the Gila was said to be its northern boundary.

The ox, in a perfectly wild state, abounds here; the guides have shot three or four. As we descended from the high ground, an immense red bull rushed by in front, at great speed; it was more novel and exciting than the sight of buffaloes.

The following day, December 3d, was passed at San Bernadino. The hope of obtaining mules of the Apaches resulted in disappointment; quite a number of them came to the camp, but none of the village which Leroux had visited; they gave information as to the route to the San Pedro, and promised a guide. They are poor, dirty Indians, but are generally dressed in cotton shirts, and many in trousers; they wear fine moccasins, with tops, or leggings attached. They ride fine horses, and are armed with formidable lances, guns and bows; they are ugly and squalid, wear their hair generally long, and in various fashions. They wear a kind of leather skull cap, now and then ornamented by feathers. They seem to understand Spanish, and no doubt speak it, imperfectly; but all Indians have a singular aversion to using, when not really necessary, any language foreign to them; their own tongue is, by far, the most brutal grunt that I have ever heard; their lips scarcely move, and the words come out a stuttering, jerking guttural.

That day, Allen—who is the only member of the battalion not a Mormon,—got back after an absence of five days; he had found our road just beyond the first descent into the pass, and his great misfortunes seem to have turned upon his taking it for granted that the command could not have come that way; he had been stripped of every thing by Indians, and, having no knife, had eaten of a dead horse, in the fashion of a wolf.

A party of pioneers worked on a Fronteras trail, as far as it should be followed,—six or eight miles, and finding water, returned. Hunting parties were sent out, and brought in at night, beef enough for five days.

December 4th.—No Indians came in, and the guides were sent forward. In the afternoon the battalion marched eight miles to the west, into a pass of a low range of hills. There is a remarkable rock one hundred feet high just back of the camp; and in front, a peak with a façade of rock apparently painted green, yellow and brown; it is the natural color combined with moss; between is a rocky basin of water, and there is some good grass. Apparently hundreds of wild cattle come here to water daily. The road which we cut to-day is much up hill, and generally through thickets of mezquit, or thorny bushes. This camp is less than twenty miles from Fronteras, Sonora.

December 5th.—The defile was long and rough; the tongue of a wagon was broken; but some of the useful parts were brought on. The condition of many of the mules may be judged from the fact that two died last night, the warmest for a month, after several days' rest, and a march of only eight miles. Fourteen miles brought me to a large spring, which as usual, is lost after running a few yards. I met the Indian guide passing back rapidly on his grey horse, bow in hand, and giving the column a wide berth. I however brought him to, and had a little talk with him in barbarous Spanish. He was very uneasy. I thought at first he had run off from Leroux. The wild cattle are very numerous. I saw one killed, but only after twenty wounds, and a number of the shots at ten paces, as sometimes with buffalo. Mr. Hall was chased by one, and put in much danger by the obstinacy of his mule. I measured the spinal process of one, ("hump rib") that was eleven inches in length.

On the 6th, the battalion cut its way twelve miles through mezquit; there was rain and some snow, so that a camp at a water hole at a fine grove of oak and walnut was very welcome. The assimilation of the wild cattle to buffalo, was further observed in the separation, most of the year, of bulls from all the rest. Cows or calves were scarcely seen, and none killed.

Next day the battalion remained in camp, and were busy smoking beef. In the evening a guide returned, reporting no water for twelve miles, but the grass unusually green, and indications of the river being not many miles beyond.

December 8th.—There was a march of seventeen miles to the north-west, and the battalion had to do without water. The valley of the San Pedro, stretching far north, gave indications that the river was very near. They passed near a field of snow. Wild horses were seen very near.

December 9th.—I marched at sunrise. As we approached a long black streak of mezquit, etc., where we imagined we should find the San Pedro, we were much disappointed. We fell into the smooth valley of a dry branch, and I finally, in my great anxiety, feared we had passed too far south for the river, or that this dry branch was the head of it; the guides had all become doubtful themselves. Troops of wild horses, cattle and antelopes, seemed to invite the attention, little of which was given. Leaving the great valley of the dry branch, we soon left behind all appearances of broken ground, mezquit or timber; taking our course toward a mountain range, which was white with snow, and from which a northwester cut us to the bone. A vast unbroken slope of prairie was before us; my anxiety became very great, and I pushed on at a fast gait to the guides, and after ascending somewhat, saw a valley indeed, but no other appearance of a stream than a few ash trees in the midst; but they, with numerous cattle paths, gave every promise of water. On we pushed, and finally, but not until within twenty paces, I saw a fine bold stream! There was the San Pedro, so long and anxiously sought. I crossed the stream without difficulty, to the other and smoother side of the valley, at noon, and camped six miles lower down. We were twenty-seven miles without water. My animals get grama grass every night on the hills; it is straw colored, and looks dead, but the mules have lately improved on it, and the thousands of wild cattle and horses are fat.

Next day the march was fifteen miles down the

river. It seemed a fertile valley, the low grounds about a mile wide; salmon trout, eighteen inches long, were caught. The wild cattle were still more numerous, and it was observed that they made dry "wallows" like the buffalo.

On the 11th, there was found very high grass in the bottom, which was also lumpy. At two o'clock, I again came to a cañon, and several men having been wounded, and much meat killed, I encamped.

There was quite an engagement with bulls, and I had to direct the men to load their muskets to defend themselves. The animals attacked in some instances without provocation, and tall grass in some places made the danger greater; one ran on a man, caught him in the thigh, and threw him clear over his body lengthwise; then it charged on a team, ran its head under the first mule and tore out the entrails of the one beyond. Another ran against a sergeant, who escaped with severe bruises, as the horns passed at each side of him; one ran at a horse tied behind a wagon, and as it escaped, the bull struck the wagon with a momentum that forced the hind part of it out of the road. I saw one rush at some pack mules, and kill one of them. I was very near Corporal Frost, when an immense coal-black bull came charging at us, a hundred yards. Frost aimed his musket, flint lock, very deliberately, and only fired when the beast was within six paces; it fell headlong, almost at our feet. One man, charged on, threw himself flat, and the bull jumped over him and passed on.

A bull, after receiving two balls through its heart, and two through the lungs, ran on a man. I have seen the heart. Lieut. Stoneman was accidentally wounded in the thumb. We crossed a pretty stream which I have named "Bull Run."

The river was followed two more days, twenty-two miles, making sixty-five in all; the ground became more difficult, with the approach to mountains extending to the Gila. Then Leroux and other guides returned from an exploration of the table-land to the west, where at twenty miles distance, they had found water, on a trail to Tucson; at it were a party of Apaches, some Mexicans distilling mezcal whiskey, and some soldiers; they reported a garrison of two hundred men at Tucson. Leroux, to get off, invented some story, and Foster, the interpreter had thought proper to go on to Tucson, to give it more probability.

The battalion were exercised in arms, and an order was read, announcing a march for Tucson; not specially to attack it, but it was necessary to "overcome all resistance."

December 14th, the battalion turned up the bluff, ascending for nine miles, when the trail was struck.

About six miles from the still-house, I ordered fifty men to follow, and pushed on with my suit, and passed the advance guard and pioneers. Coming to water, I rode in among four or five soldiers in uniform, cutting grass, their horses and arms at their saddles, near by; they seemed scarcely to notice our arrival; a strange simplicity; but indicating a conviction that the savages were their natural and only enemies.

The camp was established at dark, on good ground with water, grass and fuel. The march was twenty miles.

The sergeant of the Mexican party said that reports had been spread which alarmed the people, who were about to fly; and the commandant sent me a request not to pass through the town; that he had orders to prevent it; but that I might pass on either side. I told the sergeant, that if the garrison was very weak I should probably not molest it ; but to go back and tell the people, that we were their friends, and wanted to purchase flour, etc. He soon left.

Next day twelve miles were marched, and the camp was made, as expected, with no water; quite an obstacle was encountered in a new species of cactus, which maddened some of the mules. Four other Mexican soldiers were met, who acted in the same confiding manner, but were secured; on being questioned in camp, the corporal, a son of Comaduran the commandant, said that Foster was under guard, but had been *begged* to come with them, and refused! A note was sent by one of the pioneers, demanding Foster's return to this camp ; and adding, that the prisoners were held as hostages.

Another extraordinary variety of cactus was seen which should be called *columnar ;* a straight column thirty feet high, near two feet in diameter, fluted very similarly to the Corinthian column, only the capital wanting; some throw out one or more branches, gracefully curved and then vertical, like the branches of a candelabrum.

But two days' rations of meat had been issued in the last two weeks from the commissary provisions.

After midnight Foster was brought to camp by two officers; one was a "commissioner," authorized to make a special armistice. After a rather long conference, they were dismissed with the proposition, that a few arms should be delivered as tokens of a surrender, which only required them not to serve against the United States during the present war until exchanged.

The last camp proved to be sixteen miles from the town. A few miles out, a fine looking cavalryman well armed was met; he delivered a dispatch, and was suffered to retire without answer; it was merely a refusal of the terms offered. The battalion was made ready for engagement. Very soon after, two Mexicans were met, who gave information that the post had been evacuated, and that most of the inhabitants had also left, forced off by the military; that these last had carried off two brass cannon. But about a dozen well mounted men met and accompanied the battalion into town: some of them were said to be soldiers.

The camp was made about half a mile beyond the town, which is a Pueblo. About a hundred of the perhaps five hundred inhabitants had remained. The barracks are on the highest ground, enclosed by a wall with abutments and battlements in bad repair.

Some provisions were brought to the camp for sale; the battalion was now without salt, and only three bushels could be obtained there.

The valley of the little river, about a mile wide, seemed fertile. The wheat was then green; the only fruits observed were pomegranates and quinces. There being little or no grass, a quantity of wheat found in the forts was used for feed, and as much as could be carried, was ordered to be taken both for mules and men. A party from the garrison had been sent to the Gila, perhaps to observe the march of the battalion, expected to pass by General Kearny's route; they were reported to have passed back that afternoon, making a circuit round the Pueblo.

Next morning, many mules having strayed in the thickets, which would cover approaches to the town and camp, it was thought well to make a demonstration at least, up the little river, toward a village, eight or ten miles above; its remarkably large stone church had been visible from the hills, in approaching the town. Lieutenant Colonel Cooke, with a dozen officers and others, mounted on mules, and about forty volunteers from the battalion, accordingly passed up; but marching four or five miles, it was found that the thickets had become a dense forest of mezquit trees, which extended to the village, offering to the Mexicans an excellent ambush; and so, while waiting for the straggling footmen to close up, it was concluded that, the demonstration being made, every reasonable object except the examination of the church, was accomplished, and so the detachment returned to camp. Signal smokes had been observed, and it was afterward ascertained, that at this Indian-like announcement of the approach, the Mexicans further retreated; and the reinforcements, which had come from the presidios of Fronteras, Santa Cruz and Tubac, marched to return to their posts.

A note was written to be delivered to Captain Comaduran, on his return, enclosing a letter for Don Manuel Gandara, Governor of Sonora, at Ures, who was said to be very well disposed to the United States; it is here given:

Camp at Tucson, Sonora, Dec. 18th, 1846.

Your Excellency:—The undersigned, marching in command of a battalion of United States infantry from New Mexico to California, has found it convenient for the passage of his wagon train, to cross the frontier of Sonora. Having passed within fifteen miles of Fronteras, I have found it necessary to take this presidio in my route to the Gila.

Be assured that I did not come as an enemy of the *people* whom you represent; they have received only kindness at my hands. Sonora refused to contribute to the support of the present war against my country, alleging the excellent reasons that all her resources were necessary to her defence from the incessant attacks of savages; that the central government gave her no protection, and was therefore entitled to no support. To this might have been added that *Mexico supports a war upon Sonora.* For I have seen New Mexicans within her boundary trading for the spoil of her people, taken by murderous, cowardly Indians, who attack only to lay waste, rob and fly to the mountains; and I have certain information, that this is the practice of many years; thus one part of Mexico allies itself against another.

The unity of Sonora with the States of the north, now her neighbors, is necessary effectually to subdue these Parthian Apaches.

Meanwhile, I make a wagon road from the streams of the Atlantic to the Pacific Ocean, through the valuable plains, and mountains rich with minerals, of Sonora. This I trust will prove useful to the citizens of either republic, who, if not more closely, may unite in the pursuits of a highly beneficial commerce.

With sentiments of esteem and respect, I am your Excellency's most obedient servant,

P. St. G. Cooke,

Lieut-colonel of United States Forces.

To his Excel'y, Señ. Don Manuel Gandara.

Governor of Sonora, Ures, Sonora.

A false alarm was made that night; "at midnight I was awoke from sound sleep by one of the picket guard, who, all out of breath, assured me that a large Mexican army was coming from the town.

"Such a high-sounding announcement only aroused

dreamy thoughts of historical war, but instantly the officer of the day informed me that a picket had fired upon some body of men coming from town. My trumpets instantly rang with the "assembly." I sent a company to the village, with a reconnoitering party under Lieutenant Stoneman in advance, and other dispositions were made. But nothing was discovered."

The best information possible had been sought as to the desert between Tucson and the Gila River; it was a most formidable undertaking for the way-worn footmen.

On the 18th, the march was resumed before ten o'clock; the river sinks within a few miles; the mules were carefully watered about seven miles out, at the last water; the next three miles, down the dry bed was exceedingly difficult, from sand and otherwise. Leaving the course of the stream, the level ground offered much obstruction in mezquit; at dusk more sand was encountered; after that the march was continued three hours over a level baked-clay surface, with a few mezquit thickets. In one of these the camp was made at nine o'clock P.M. without water. There was no moon. The march had been twenty-four miles. The mules were tied up and scantily fed with wheat.

The march was resumed the 20th, at sunrise; it was fourteen miles to the pass between two isolated small mountains, and a water hole, reported to be there, could not be found. There was nothing to do but march on; there was the same baked-clay surface, with a little sand. At sundown a very small pool was come to; too shallow for dipping with a cup, but enough for most of the men to get a drink by lying down.

At 7 o'clock, after dark, permission was given to the captains to halt their companies at discretion, but not over six hours in all. The mules would certainly go on better in the cold night without water.

At 8.30 o'clock the advance guard, who had been with the guides, were overtaken; they had stopped at a small pool, but the loose and packed mules, which had been sent on, had rushed into it and consumed or spoiled all. Just then an agreed signal of sufficient water was observed, a fire made of dry artemisia. The march was continued; it was cloudy and very dark; after advancing a mile or two with difficulty over very uneven and bushy ground the fire was reached, and found to have been made by a stupid guide for his own comfort. The mules could go no further over such ground, and a halt for the rest of the night was ordered.

The battalion had then marched twenty-six hours of the last thirty-six; they were almost barefooted, carried their muskets and knapsacks; the mules had worked forty-seven miles without water. A little wheat was now given to them.

The march was resumed at 7 o'clock A. M.; the guides well ahead.

The road was very bad; after three or four hours Leroux was met, with information of some pools three or four miles on; he was sent on again to search further. At 11 o'clock, part of the battalion arrived there; sentinels were posted to prevent dipping, and one pool was reserved for the beeves. (When they reached it, they rushed in headlong, spoiling all.)

Weaver, a guide, had reason to believe it was eighteen miles further to the river; the temperature was almost hot;—but soon, Leroux came again, to illume the gloomy prospect by the happy announcement of a sufficiency of rain ponds a mile or two on; and there, soon after noon, the battalion arrived and camped; and there was mezquit for the animals to browse. The guides were sent on.

This great plain of clay, sand and gravel, with artemisias and mezquit, seems unbounded to the west. I am told it extends a hundred miles; with no water or animals; but in the dim distance unconnected fantastically shaped mountains appear. It is a gold district, and reputed to be of the very richest; but never yet worked, on account of its utter barrenness, and the fear of Indians.

I have been mounted thirty-two of the last fifty-two hours; and what with midnight conferences, alarms and marches, have had little rest for five days.

The battalion have marched sixty-two miles from Tucson, in about fifty-one hours; no ration of meat was issued yesterday.

December 21*st*.—The battalion marched at sunrise; the road was very good, and passed between two small mountains, where the columnar cactus abounded; a decayed one showed a framework of wooden poles, cylindrically disposed, and evidently suitable for shafts for lance or spear; the old columns for some feet above the ground have a bark, and exactly the appearance of the cottonwood.

We were soon gladdened at sight of the trees of the Gila; but the trail bending westward, approached it obliquely, and we found it ten miles to its bank. We had struck Gen. Kearny's route, and here went into camp.

From the point where Gen. Kearny left the Rio Grande, about two hundred and twenty eight miles below Sante Fè, and where our routes diverged, to their camp, near the Pimo village, I made a map and sketch of my road; I had the aid of no instrument but a compass.

Captain Emory of the Topographical Engineers, on the General's staff, had the duty of making a map with the aid, of course, of the best instruments, for determining latitude, longitude, etc. My rude map covered four hundred and seventy-four miles, and it chanced to get into Captain Emory's hands while he was finishing his own map in Washington. The tests which he was able to apply to it, proved its singular accuracy, and he incorporated it with his own. It appears in atlases as "Colonel Cooke's wagon route."

The treaty of peace and boundaries with Mexico established the Gila River as a boundary between the two countries. A new administration, in which southern interests prevailed, with the great problem of the practicability and best location of a Pacific Railroad under investigation, had the map of this wagon route before them, with its continuance to the west, and perceived that it gave exactly the solution of its unknown element; that a southern route would avoid both the Rocky Mountains and Sierra Nevada, with their snows, and would meet no obstacle in this great interval. The new "Gadsden Treaty" with Mexico was the result; it was signed December 30th, 1853.

Accordingly it is found that the new boundary agreed upon, is constituted chiefly of arbitrary right lines; the most southern one being nearly a tangent of the southern bend of the road.

This most costly acquisition of parts of Sonora and Chihuahua became an important part of the New Territory, which received the name of Arizona.

Before we arrived here, although eight miles above the Pimo village, there were many Indians on the ground, and they have since flocked into camp, some mounted, and bring small sacks of corn, flour, beans, etc. One brought me letters from General Kearny and Major Swords, Quarter-master, which mention eleven broken down mules and two bales of Indian goods left for me with the Pimos. Being informed that there is very little corn at the villages, the guides were directed to open trade here; but they reported the prices such, that they could do nothing; and I have forbidden individuals to trade for corn or wheat until further orders.

Many of these Indians, I was somewhat surprised to see, are nearly naked; they manufacture cotton blankets, and show every desire to be clothed; they are good looking and very lively; they know nothing of the value of money, and little of weights and measures; their language is a pleasant one. A few speak the Spanish, and I was surprised to see one, who spoke it well, have recourse to his fingers to explain the subtraction of five mules, dead, from the eleven left for me.

The weather is like early October in New Mexico; warm days and cold nights. Cottonwoods, the only tree here, are only partially yellowed by frosts.

I have conversed with the principal chief, Juan Antonio, and he and another have supped with me. He said the commander of Tucson sent to demand the mules and Indian goods left with him; that he refused, and declared he would resist force with force. He said I could see they were poor and naked, but they were content to live here by hard work on the spot which God had given them; and not like others to rob or steal; that they did not fear us, and run like the Apaches, because they made it a rule to injure no one in any way, and therefore never expected any one to injure them. In fact the Apaches do not molest them; but it is owing to experience of their prowess.

I have spoken to the two senior captains of the battalion on the subject of their settling near here; they seem to look upon it favorably. Captain Hunt asked my permission to talk to the chief on the subject, and I approved of it.

The Pimos are large and fine looking, seem well fed, ride good horses, and are variously clothed, though many have only the centre cloth; the men and women have extraordinary luxuriance and length of hair. With clean white blankets and streaming hair, they present mounted quite a fine figure. But innocence and cheerfulness are their most distinctive characteristics. I am told the Mexican officers used every persuasion, and promise of plunder, to excite hostility toward us.

A few bushels of sweet corn were bought, and issued as rations.

December 22d, the march was resumed. Several miles short of the village, groups of men, women and girls were met, coming to welcome the battalion; " These last, naked generally above the hips, were of every age and pretty, walking often by twos with encircling arms; it was a gladdening sight, so much cheerfulness and happiness. One little girl particularly, by a fancied resemblance, interested me much; she was so joyous that she seemed very pretty and innocent; I could not resist tying on her head, as a turban, a bright new silk handkerchief, which I happened to wear to-day; the effect was beautiful to see—a picture of happiness!"

The camp is full of the Indians, and a great many have some eatables, including watermelons, to trade; and they seem only to want clothing or cotton cloth, and beads. I am sorry they will be disappointed. It reminds me of a crowded New Orleans market. There must be two thousand in camp, all enjoying themselves very much; they stroll about, their arms around each other, graceful and admirable in form; their language certainly sounds like ours; their honesty is perfect!

The march was resumed the 23d. At the chief's house I stopped a few minutes; I told him I had seen many tribes, and that the Pimos were the happiest and most prosperous I had ever seen; that as long as they adhered to their principles of industry, honesty, peace and cheerful content, they would continue so; that while they never injured their neighbors, their true safety lay in uniting to resist vigorously every aggression; that wishing them well, I desired to add to their comfort and welfare by introducing sheep among them, by giving him for the ultimate use of his people, three ewes with young, which was the best I could do.

I received to-day a letter from General Kearny, written at Warner's rancho, California; indicating that his arrival was very important, not only to the welfare of California, but to its conquest.

The march was fifteen miles. The whole distance was through cultivated grounds, and a luxuriantly rich soil; there is a very large zequia well out from the river; the plain appeared to extend in every direction fifteen or twenty miles. The camp was made at the village of the Maricopas; notwithstanding a different language, all that has been said of the Pimos is applicable to them. They live in cordial amity, and their habits, agriculture and manufactures are the same, as also their religion, which consists in a simple belief in a great over-ruling spirit. This seems to have proved a foundation for a most enviable practical morality. Don Jose Messio is their governor, and their population is estimated as high as ten thousand. Their dwellings are dome shaped wicker work, thatched with straw or cornstalks, and from twenty to fifty feet in diameter; in front is usually a large arbor, on which is piled the cotton in the pod, for drying; horses, mules, oxen, chickens and dogs seem to be the only domestic animals; they have axes, hoes, shovels, and harrows. The soil is so easily pulverized, as to make the plow unnecesssry.

Busy preparations were made for the march about noon next day, to encounter a jornada of above forty miles, caused by a great bend of the river with mountains. The rations were found to have suffered great loss or wastage; of the beeves many were in good order, and three of the oxen were still left. A few exchanges for fatter animals were made, the pack saddles in excess of twelve to a company, were disposed of. Eight mules, abandoned by the General, had been picked up by the Maricopas, and were delivered to me.

The hospitality and generosity of these allied tribes is noted; they feed and assist in every way travelers who are in need; fortunately, perhaps, these have been few. I observed them parching grain in a basket, by throwing in live coals and keeping all in motion, by tossing into the air.

They have the simplicity of nature, and none of the affected reserve and dignity characteristic of other Indians, before whites. At the sound of a trumpet, playing of a violin, the killing of a beef, they rush to see and hear, with delight or astonishment strongly exhibited.

About a half bushel of corn was procured for each animal, and three days' rations of corn meal.

December 25*th*.—The march was up hill, and the

road rather sandy. Half an hour before sundown, having long seen Leroux's smoke, indicating he had found grass, I pushed on to examine the ground before dark; I stationed the sentinels so that the mules could be turned loose in the mezquit, without much danger of their escaping to seek water. The wagons arrived at 8 o'clock, the march having been eighteen miles. The weather has been quite warm for several days, but fortunately, as there is no water, it was cloudy this afternoon.

Next morning, with reveille at 4.30 o'clock, the battalion could not be got in motion much before 7. Some rough, difficult ground was found in the gap of the ridge, which consumed much time. I then rode ahead and reached the river about sunset. The guides had preceded me, and following their path, (a wrong one) I passed through a very uneven willow-grown bottom of the river and found them taking their ease at the water-edge, with some yellow, broken, years-old grass near, which had been their attraction, as " the best the country afforded."

I selected a camp-ground, and marked it by little fires, made by some packmen, who had arrived. The wagons came about 7.30.

The river is here brackish; this is caused by the Saline River, a larger stream than the Gila above, which flows into it below the Maricopa village. The day's march had been twenty-three miles.

Here I relieved the train of three hundred mule shoes, and the nails, by making a "cache;" which in far western language, means burying valuables in the ground, and noting by some permanent object, the exact position.

For the next six days the marches averaged ten miles. It was an unremitting struggle with the rude barrenness of a rainless wilderness. Once, the mule drove was sent four miles to some grass which the guides had reported, but which was found to be nearly worthless; Weaver said, it sprang up from a shower which fell there four years ago, as he knew; (but the duration of a cycle of these phenomena unfortunately he could not determine.) The animals existed on corn, doled by the pint, with now and then flag grass, and willow bushes on the river margin and sand-bars. Many miles of road were beaten, with much dust, in a clay formation, where mule tracks were six inches deep; much sand was encountered, and several volcanic bluffs, which required much labor to be made passable.

The second of these days, we met two travelers, a Chilean and a California refugee; they gave very confused information of a renewed state of war in California, and of bodies of armed men, with droves coming to Sonora. They had passed another small party a few days before.

The same day Leroux and four other guides, and Mr. Hall were sent forward, with dispatches; and they were instructed to send back information of any thing observed on the route, of importance to the expedition. They were also ordered to bring fresh mules and beeves to meet the battalion as early as possible. One of them was required to be at Warner's rancho, when the battalion should arrive there, about "January 21st."

January 1st, 1847.—Cottonwood-bark and branches, and mezquit, were added yesterday to the forage list. Many of the animals, including sheep, have appeared to be poisoned; a few have died, the others appear to be gradually recovering.

Whenever there is a bed where the river sometimes flows, we find more or less grass; there is little doubt that only want of rain prevents its growth elsewhere; but the bottoms frequently show salty efflorescences; also much of it seems of mere clay, which I *think* will not produce vegetation.

We found in this night's camp a party described by the Mexicans whom we met, including a lady who was delivered of a fine child two days ago; and she traveled yesterday ten miles on horseback. They report the wells in the desert, of which the General wrote, to be dried up—probably filled partly with sand.

I am now preparing a boat of the two ponton wagon-bodies lashed together, end to end, between two dry cottonwood logs; in this I shall put all the baggage I can risk. The river is rapid, and in places three or four feet deep; and here it is one hundred and fifty yards wide. I have determined to send Lieutenant Stoneman in charge; he professes to have had similar experience, and is desirous to undertake it.

January 6th.—In five days but fifty-four miles of progress has been made, and after much anxiety the ponton boat, now first seen, has joined the battalion empty! The experiment proved a failure, and the stores have been landed in several places; but three or four inches of water was to be found on several rapids.

Parties with pack mules have been out all the time striving to meet the boat, and recover at least the flour, from its load of two thousand five hundred pounds of provisions and corn. And these have not been heard from!

It was found necessary for our wagons to vary much from General Kearny's trail; and a road was cut, in places, through miles of dense thickets, etc.

Next day only seven miles could be made; points of stony ridges and clay gullies required much work.

The mules were ordered to be sent across the river to browse in the young willows, flag-grass, etc., and it turned out they had to swim.

January 8th.—Sixteen miles took the battalion to the mouth of the Gila.

"A vast bottom; the country about the two rivers is a picture of desolation; nothing like vegetation beyond the alluvium of the two rivers; bleak mountains, wild looking peaks, stony hills and plains, fill the view. We are encamped in the midst of wild hemp. The mules are in mezquit thickets, with a little bunch grass, a half a mile off."

January 9th.—We marched very early. The wagons were six hours reaching the crossing of the Colorado; about half of the road was bad, sand or soft clay; the pioneers did much work. The mules are weak, and their failing, or flagging to-day in ten miles, is very unpromising for the hundred mile stretch, dry and barren, before them. There is no grass, and only scanty cottonwood boughs for them to-night, but I sent out forty men to gather the fruit, called tornia, of a variety of the mezquit. They have gathered twelve or fifteen bushels, which has been spread out to be eaten on a hard part of the sand-bar.

Francisco was sent across the river to fire the thickets beyond—this to clear the way for the pioneer party in the morning. He says the river is deeper than usual; it is wider than the Missouri, and of the same muddy color. It is probable that sugar-cane may be cultivated here.

It is said to be sixty miles to tide water, and one hundred and sixty to the mouth of the river.

January 10th.—The mules were driven two miles to grass; some of the pack mule party arrived bringing four hundred and fifty pounds of flour; a

·part of them had been left, hunting for another deposit. The companies were ordered to cross with their baggage, in the ponton boat, leaving empty wagons, teamsters and mules; the ford inclining down the river, was above a mile long and in two channels.

The battalion continued crossing with great difficulty all the night, the water in some places almost too deep to use a pole. The sheep were now doing better; lately a few had been left each day, and only one hundred and thirty remained.

"*January* 11*th,* 9 *p. m.*—With my mind full of anxiety, I force myself to the task of recording the deeds of the day. I am in camp at the 'well,' fifteen miles from the river crossing; I resolved that here the battalion *should* come to-day, and for these reasons: I had not rations or time, under the probable state of affairs in California, to spend another day beyond the river; there was nothing for the mules on this side, and as they must graze on that side, and must pull the wagons over when they came, there would be little less to do to-morrow than to-day.

The first difficulty I encountered this morning

was, that instead of the boat being in readiness to cross the sheep at five o'clock, as ordered, it was not over until quarter past seven; then I had all the baggage of the field and staff taken to it in ten minutes, and crossed myself, taking in addition ten of the men.

I was then told by the adjutant, that many loads of company baggage had still to be brought over; the round trips had averaged an hour and a half, and on all sides their idea of the impossibility of making the set day's journey was conveyed to me. I ordered that the rest of the baggage should come over in the wagons, the sheep only should be ferried; the remaining baggage was then loaded accordingly; the mules had been driven in at daylight, and I got the wagons started in the river at eight o'clock. The river runs swiftly and is at least four feet deep. About nine, I got to where the battalion had encamped. Here in willow bushes, which concealed everything, I found all in confusion; tents standing, every man doing his own pleasure, some eating, some cooking. Time was flying fast. I then saw a wagon, the only one of Company C, standing half way across, with mules taken out on a sand bar, and nothing apparently doing. Half an hour later, its commander reported to me that they were stuck, etc., and could not get out. I told him they were not trying, that they had the same opportunities as the others, (the boat had been used turn about,) that other wagons had got over easily, and men in them against positive orders; that I should march immediately, and would not help him.

Meanwhile the boat came, half loaded with men and baggage, and with less than a third of the sheep, and instantly the crew disappeared. I had almost to force, personally, men into the boat to take it back. They then spent half an hour in water deeper than they could reach with their ten foot poles. So bad seemed the chance of getting over more than another load, that I sent word to Lieutenant Smith to bring over the boat full of the best sheep, and the others might be abandoned if they could not swim. Quite a number of mules had fallen and been drowned; the river had an inch of ice, where there was no current. Then I forced off the battalion, at 10 o'clock, to march fifteen miles of bad road, leaving a company in the river, and two-thirds of the sheep on the other side. I knew these last were in good hands, and that the company would be excited to do their best. The first mile was ascending, and through deep sand; the mules were torpid and sullen. The prospect of getting to this camp was almost desperate. I gave orders that private mules should be put to the wagons; then, if necessary, to leave a wagon on the road. Two were thus left. I rode on and stopped all pack and loose animals at a patch of mezquit, the tornia or fruit of which had fallen to the ground, until all the wagons had passed. The fire of the pioneer party raged around us. [I sent twenty men on, to collect mezquit beans or tornia, believing the battalion would arrive after dark; I knew there was no grass.] (I arrived at four o'clock, and was met by a man who told me 'there was not a drop of water.' The worse prospect for sixty miles ahead, instantly rose to frighten me for the three hundred and sixty nearly worn out footmen, who confide all to me.)

I found the party digging most energetically, not only at the old well, but they had commenced another. Soon, in the first, they struck damp sand, and so on, to water. When the quicksands were struck, they caved in so as to render it impossible to get water more than two or three inches deep. Many expedients were discussed; it was considered that our only hope was in a wash-tub belonging to the wife of a captain. The new well progressed slowly through hard clay. The first wagon came at sunset; at dusk the tub arrived. Lieutenant Oman reported to me, to my astonishment, that they were unwilling to give up that valuable article!—upon which our lives seemed to depend. I had it taken. The well then seemed for some time to work promisingly. Then it failed. I had the tub taken up, and the bottom, which had been bored, knocked out; then it worked better. It was late however and anxious expectants thronged the hole. I was seated in my tent, consulting with the guides, when Lieutenant Oman reported that the well had failed worse than ever.

My doubts seemed converted to the certainty of evil and disaster. I then learned that the company I had left were camped six miles back; their team having given out.

I sent for Weaver to inquire of the route, long thought of, to follow the river some sixty miles down; he so represented the country as to give scarce a hope of its practicability under our circumstances. Once more I went to the well, and ordered a fresh detail to be put on the new one: they had found in ten feet only mud, and its upper surface was two feet lower than the old one, which was ten feet deep. I then with my mind full of trouble, sat down to write. In half an hour, Lieut. O. came and reported that in the new well, he had 'come to water that could be dipped with a camp kettle.' It was like a great light bursting upon darkness and gloom.

I am writing with effort to suppress feeling. This well failing, what had I to expect of the next, which I knew to be dry now, and not, like this, deriving its supply from a great river, and to be only reached by going without water for a night and two days, in addition to this hard day; and the next hope of water almost three of our average marches still further on; and *behind*, starvation and failure.)

(But my faith had not failed, for, at the worst, I gave orders for a beef to be slaughtered at daylight, to be cooked before ten o'clock, and other

8*

preparations for the night following without water. The sheep were all got over.)

Many mules gave out to-day, and at best the prospect is bad; not only want of water, but so very little for the poor animals to eat. I had five bushels of tornia brought here by each company.

It is half past ten o'clock at night; I have ordered Lieut. O. with twelve picked men to go through to-morrow to the Alamo Mocho, to dig and prepare for us.

(Eighteen hours of unceasing labor has been my lot to-day, with anxiety enough to turn one grey. Our safety seems the accident of a pocket of clay— which served as a wall—reaching below the level of quicksand, which probably extends from the bed of the river.")

In the morning it took from 9 to 11.30 o'clock, to water the mules of three companies; then the march began, leaving the others to follow, when their mules were well watered. A guide had stopped at some scant straw colored "grass," and camp was made about sundown. It was a wilderness of sand, mixed with gravel and small stones;

the only vegetable production a slim bush, which the New Mexicans call "stinking wood."

The 13th, the march was commenced at sunrise ; it was a hot day, and some bad sand was encountered. It was thirteen miles to the wells, and the battalion arrived at two o'clock. The advance party had improved an old well, and dug another; there was only mezquit without fruit. "Now after eight hours, the watering is still going on ; the poor animals after drinking the impure warm water, seem unsatisfied, and have to be driven away to the bushes on which to browse."

Next day signal smokes were frequently seen ; believed to be made by Indians; a small party would have seen enough of them. It was about twenty-five miles to another old well, the *Pozo Hondo;* and Lieutenant Stoneman with twenty-five men and Weaver were sent early in the morning to go through and prepare for the battalion.

The corporal and two men, who against instructions, remained seeking more flour, left by the boat, had not yet come up; and two more men were missing since leaving the Colorado.

. "I had lately a conversation with old Weaver,

which was not official. He said, 'the Tontos live in that range over there; I never see them with more than one or two lodges together; they are a band of the Coyoteros, and are called fools for their ignorance. When I went over, once, from the Pimos to the Cochanos and Mochabas, I met some lodges and had a fuss with them.'—'What sort?'—'Oh, we killed two or three and burnt their lodges, and took all the women and children and sold them.' 'What!' 'Yes, I have often caught the women and children of the Digger Indians and sold them in New Mexico and Sonora. They bring a hundred dollars. Mr. —, of Tucson told me a squaw I sold him, ran off, and was found dead, famished for water I s'pose, going over from the Pimos to the Colorado.' 'What, have you no feeling for her death, trying to return to her father and mother you tore her from?' 'I killed her father and mother, as like as not; they stole all our traps; as fast as we could stick a trap in the river, they'd come and steal it, and shoot arrows into our horses; they thought we would leave them for them to eat, but we built a big fire and burnt them up.'"

This Alamo Mocho (broken cottonwood) well is

near the foot of a very steep bank, perhaps eighty feet down to a remarkable depression of great extent and as wide as a great river; and most likely it is the bed of one, or of a dried up creek of the Gulf. The flat bottom is grown up with mezquit. (Two or three years after this date, a stream suddenly broke through, or made its appearance, much to the joy of some travelers; it is called New River.)

January 14*th*.—The march began at 11 A. M: details had been at work the whole night, and up to that hour, drawing the scant water for mules and cattle; and it was found necessary to leave two wagons.

Some bad sand was encountered this day; sometimes only a little, blown from sand hills, which were skirted; then a great flat of baked clay, which had evidently been covered by water, on which the animals scarcely left a track. The battalion observed the tracks of hundreds of mules and horses; herds believed to have been driven within a few months to Sonora. Sea shells, and salt, found on this great plain, indicate that it was once the bottom of the Gulf.

Having marched seventeen miles, the battalion

came at dark to a mezquit thicket, and camped
There was no water.

Marching at sunrise, next day, seven miles over the flat broken plain, brought them to the Pozo Hondo. "The distant mountains to our left and front were mingled with clouds; the rising sun painted all with bright and varied hues, and then we saw the distinct colors of a rainbow. . . which only once before have we seen, in the other desert of Tucson."

Here were met fresh mules and some beeves, sent under charge of one guide; twenty-two of fifty-seven mules had been lost. There was great disappointment in the well; the water was issued by the gill; it was necessary to go on; a fat beef was killed and cooked; and the work of catching with the lazo, and harnessing the new mules, many of which were as wild as deer, and had to be thrown down, consumed the whole delay of near three hours; one mule, after being harnessed, broke away from three stout men, and ran off at great speed into the desert, unfollowed.

Here was heard the distressing news of a disastrous engagement of General Kearny; of his wounds, and of the death of valued and loved officers, and many other dragoons. Captains Johnston and Moore and Lieutenant Hammond had fallen.

Eleven more miles were marched, and halt was then made until 2 o'clock A. M.; the mules were kept tied, and some bunch grass was cut and fed to them.

"Besides being nearly starved, our mules have had no water since yesterday morning; the men too, are without it; it is necessary to go on in the cold night, speedily to end this terrible state of things; the ten miles of much dreaded sand is before us."

At 2 A. M., January 16th the march was resumed.

"I had a large advance guard and all the guides on duty, telling Weaver not to lose sight of the leading wagon; it was starlight. Four miles from our bivouac I stopped until all had passed, and found that even then a team or two had apparently given out. I gave various orders of relief, transferred mules, etc.; toward daylight it was exceedingly cold, too much so to ride; then the guides got lost, and, by their not obeying strictly my orders, the wagons lost at least a mile; here the new teams seemed almost exhausted; two companies had lost harness and I managed to find some other for them. I found the road was about to prove much longer than I had been informed. About 10 o'clock in the morning as usual, it became of summer heat. Finally, near eleven, I reached, with the foremost wagon, the first water of the Cariza;—a clear running stream gladdened the eyes, after the anxious dependence on muddy wells for five or six days. One company, which met with an accident, was so far delayed into the heat of the day, that the mules entirely failed several miles off; a new team had to be sent, and the wagon came up at sunset. I found the march to be nineteen miles; thus without water for near three days, (for the working animals) and camping two nights, *in succession*, without water, the battalion made in forty-eight hours, four marches, of eighteen, eight, eleven and nineteen miles, suffering from frost, and from summer heat. Considering this, it seems certain that the fifty-six miles from Alamo Mocho, could have been made without great loss in no other way;—the divisions of time for rest, the stop only for a drink and refreshment of meat in the heat of the day, and the cold night marches.

We contented ourselves to-day, with a breakfast at 1 o'clock A. M. The sheep, I fear, are many miles back. A ration of two and a half pounds of fat beef was issued this evening.

The grass here is dry and salty. The loss of mules appears to be sixteen in the two days; our great help has been twenty-two of the General's old mules, which were watered yesterday, ' to clean out the well' before my arrival, (there was a wolf's carcass in it;) but little more water rose after that. A great many of my men are wholly without shoes, and use every expedient, such as rawhide moccasins and sandals, and even wrapping their feet in pieces of woolen and cotton cloth."

January 17*th*.—Owing to stray mules, the march was late; about mid-day the battalion reached Palm Spring, where there is a clump of twenty or thirty palm trees; but there being no grass, it was necessary to go on, and the march was fifteen miles to a place called Bajiocito, a wet swampy valley, with willow bushes, bad rank grass and no fuel; the road was up the dry bed of a mountain torrent, between mountains, ash-colored and utterly barren. "That this fifteen miles of very bad road was accomplished under the circumstances, by mules or men, is extraordinary. The men arrived here completely worn down; they staggered as they marched, as they did yesterday. The sheep are not up, but near. It is astonishing to consider what the wild young mules performed and endured; driven thirty miles to meet me, then next day, in its heat, to go through the terrible process of being broken to harness—two hours of the most violent struggles possible; then to draw wagons two marches, and thus without food, to march the third day without water."

January 18*th.*—Some of the men did not find strength to reach camp before daylight this morning. The sheep did not come up until after mid-day; there are eighty-eight left. I went through the companies this morning; they were eating their last four ounces of flour; of sugar and coffee, there has been none for some weeks. I have remaining only five public wagons, there are three, private property.

The Indian Alcalde of San Phillipi, brought me a letter, but three days old, from Commander Montgomery of the Portsmouth, and governor of San Diego; he writes that my party arrived on the 14th instant, welcomes my approach, promises refreshment, etc., for the battalion.

The Alcalde, and his interpreter, also a San Phillipian Indian, are fine looking men, nearly naked, hair long, and faces painted in red spots; their language seems a bad one, somewhat resembling that of the Apaches.

The men, who this morning were prostrate, worn out, hungry, heartless, have recovered their spirits to-night, and are singing and playing the fiddle.

With confused information of hostilities, the march was resumed the 19th, with more military order, and with baggage in the rear. The guides had reported a good firm road, with a rather narrow cañon, etc. After marching three or four miles, up hill, I came to advance guard pioneers and guides, at a standstill. Weaver coolly remarked, "I believe we are penned up;" there was a rugged ridge in front, some two hundred feet high; I ordered him to find a crossing, or I should send a company who would soon do it. With much active work, I got the wagons over in about an hour and a half. Then up the dry bed of a mountain stream, I came to the cañon and found it much worse than I had been led to expect; there were many rocks to surmount, but the worst was the narrow pass. Setting the example myself, there was much work done on it before the wagons came; the rock was hewn with axes to increase the opening. I thought it wide enough, and going on, found a hill to be ascended, to avoid a still narrower pass, with a great rock to be broken, before it could be crossed. But when a trial was made, at the first pass, it was found too narrow by a foot of solid rock. More work was done, and several trials made. The sun was now only an hour high, and it was about seven miles to the first water. I had a wagon taken to pieces, and carried through.

Meanwhile, we still hewed and hammered at the mountain side; but the best road tools had been lost in the boat experiment. The next wagon body was lifted through, and then the running gear, by lifting one side; then I rode on again, and saw a wagon up the very steep hill, and down again to the cañon. The work on the pass was perseveringly continued, and the last two wagons were pulled through by the mules, with loads undisturbed.

We had ascended the main ridge by sunset,

where a guide met me, and pointed to another a mile or two in front, and said it was very bad, and could only be passed by daylight. As there was unusually good grass, I camped; but there had been no provision made for their unexpected privation of water.

After a very cold night, with very little fuel, the march was next morning continued before sunrise; the wagons were got over the second ridge, by the help of ropes. A good descending road for seven miles then led to San Phillippi, which was found to be a small deserted Indian village. The mules were grazed, and two beeves killed for breakfast; there was no other food. In the afternoon the battalion ascended the pass of another low mountain seven miles, and had water, but very scant grass for a camp. The battalion during the march was exercised in a prairie, waiting for the wagons to come up.

The guide Charboneaux returned that day; the Governor of San Diego detaining Leroux and Mr. Hall, the road being very unsafe from hostile Californians.

The battalion was under orders to march to San Diego, and communication with General Kearny was now cut off. By the best information, the enemy were concentrated at Los Angeles. The General was marching on it from the south, and Lieutenant-Colonel Fremont approaching from the north; so that a direct march on Los Angeles from the east was evidently the proper course; and especially so, as Captain Montgomery had written, January 15th, that it was generally believed that parties of Californians, headed by leaders who had broken their paroles, would endeavor to effect a retreat to Sonora, rather than submit to our arms.

Also, the district to be thus passed through was that of the most influential and most hostile natives, and of numerous Indians, many of whom were said to be employed, or forced into their ranks by the enemy.

It was determined to take the direct road to Los Angeles; and the guides were sent to Warner's, to collect mules, etc.

One of the five missing adventurers after the lost flour, came up to that camp reporting all safe, but broken down at Bajiocito, with above four hundred pounds of flour. Assistance was sent to them. A captain reported that the two men who stopped at the river and had joined the corporal, probably misunderstood him, as giving them permission. Such things happen among volunteers.

"*January* 21*st*.—A cold cloudy morning, threatening snow. I found the path over the low mountain pass smooth and not difficult; the path, now a road, winds amid a forest of large evergreen oaks. Cold as it was, the fresh deep green grass was springing up every where from the ground. This mountain divides the waters of the Colorado and the Gulf from those which run west to the ocean. The highest ridges are crowned with pine, and we saw some snow among them. I descended rapidly to the lower slopes, and there drilled my battalion again, while the baggage closed up."

The battalion reached the rancho early, and camped.

Mr. Warner's information, at this time, placed the insurgents at or near Los Angeles, hard pressed and likely to be encountered on the road, passing here, to Sonora. It was found necessary to rest the 22d. (It is remarkable that the battalion arrived at Warner's the day that the guides were instructed, December 28th, to meet it there.) At this time was commenced the issue of four pounds of fresh meat a day, that being the only food.

"*January 22d.*—A fine April morning, for Missouri or Virginia; a frost however, and a cold night. This is a beautiful little valley, shut in by mountains or high hills on every side, the country is verdant, some large cottonwoods are leafless, but the mistletoe has lent them a green drapery.

"The name, Agua Caliente, comes from a bold stream, issuing from rock fissures at the temperature of 170°; it now sends up little clouds of steam for half a mile below. The valley, a mile long, is elliptical, and its green smooth surface really oval; at its centre stands a wonderful evergreen oak, its boughs reaching a circle, five feet above the ground, and ninety feet in diameter; the hot stream runs round one side, a cold one around the other. The Indians, of cold nights, select spots below the spring, of agreeable temperature to sleep lying in the stream, with the sod bank for a pillow."

There were a number of San Luis Indians at Warner's; they had brought here a short time before, and killed ten or eleven Californians; but they had lost thirty-eight of their tribe in the Temecala valley, killed in an ambush by Californians, and Indians of another tribe. They sought now to accompany the battalion to bury the bodies. This was conceded, and Antonio, a chief, was engaged, with ten of his men mounted, to serve as scouts and guides, and to collect and drive cattle for the subsistence of the battalion.

On the 23d of January, before marching, a talk was held with Baupista, an important chief of Cohuillos, a tribe of some two thousand Indians; and it was a rather independent band of them, that, with the Californians, defeated the San Luis tribe. He was warmly counseled as to the folly of taking any part against Americans, who would soon and forever govern the country, etc., etc.

About eighteen miles were marched; the hills were found very steep for a wagon road, and it rained several hours in the afternoon. The corporal and party came up with the flour, at this camp. He said he "did not dare to come up without it!"

The rain continued twenty-four hours; the battalion had fallen upon the rainy season. All the tents were blown down in the night; the ill-clad battalion were drenched, and suffered much. A number of mules died, and many strayed, and Antonio was found very useful in recovering them. In the afternoon, a warmer and less exposed camp was found, only three or four miles on.

The morning of January 25th was very bright; the battalion marched over the hills twelve miles into the Temecala valley. The Indians there collected before its arrival, to bury their dead, showed in the distance such military array as to be mistaken for California enemies, and preparations for a combat were made before the truth was made known.

There an official dispatch was received, announcing General Kearny's return to San Diego, and showing that the battalion was expected there, as originally ordered.

Accordingly, a cross road presenting itself, next morning the march was directed toward the San Diego mission. The San Luis, a little river generally dry, was found full of quicksand, and difficult to pass. After a seven hours' march, camp was established in its beautiful valley, near a rancho. It was now found necessary to issue five pounds of beef as a ration.

The 27th the road passed several ranchos, found deserted; then near the important old mission of San Luis Rey. The road wound through smooth green valleys, and over very lofty hills, equally smooth and green. From the top of one of these hills, was caught the first and a magnificent view of the great ocean; and by rare chance perhaps, it was so calm that it shone as a mirror.*

The day's march was sixteen miles. The previous night the herd of cattle had mostly escaped, and orders were given for its increase while marching; in consequence, the zealous irregulars drove to this camp several hundred.

* The charming and startling effect, under our circumstances, of this first view of the ocean could not be expressed; but in an old diary,—once sunk and lost in a river—I find what follows:

"I caught my first sight of the ocean, as smooth as a mirror, and reflecting the full blaze of the declining sun; from these sparkling green hill-tops it seemed that the lower world had turned to impalpable dazzling light, while by contrast, the clear sky looked dim!

"We rode on into a valley which was near, but out of view of the sea; its smooth sod was in sunlight and shade; a gentle brook wound through it; the joyous lark, the gay blackbird, the musical bluebird, even the household wren, warbled together the evening song; it seemed a sweet domestic scene which must have touched the hearts of my rude, far wanderers. But coming to us so suddenly, there was a marvellous accompaniment;—the fitful roar of tide and surf upon a rock-bound shore; while now and then some great roller burst upon the rocks with a booming thunder. It was not a discord!"

That night there was so much dew that the tents seemed wet by a rain; there was also some little frost.

Next day a march of seven and a half hours was made to San Diegetto.

January 29*th.*—The battalion passed into the Solidad Valley; and then, by cross roads over high hills, miry from rain, into a firm regular road, and sixteen miles in all, to the mission of San Diego.

" The buildings being dilapidated, and in use by some dirty Indians, I camped the battalion on the flat below. There are around us extensive gardens and vineyards, wells and cisterns, more or less fallen into decay and disorder; but also olive and picturesque date trees flourishing and ornamental. There is no fuel for miles around, and the dependence for water is some rather distant pools in the sandy San Diego, which runs (sometimes) down to the ocean. The evening of this day of the march, I rode down, by moonlight, and reported to the General in San Diego.

The battalion seemed to have deserved, and cheered heartily the following order:

HEADQUARTERS MORMON BATTALION.
Mission of San Diego, January 30, 1847.

ORDERS NO. 1.

The Lieutenant-Colonel commanding congratulates the battalion on their safe arrival on the shore of the Pacific Ocean, and the conclusion of their march of over two thousand miles.

History may be searched in vain for an equal march of infantry. Half of it has been through a wilderness where nothing but savages and wild beasts are found, or deserts where, for want of water, there is no living creature. There, with almost hopeless labor we have dug deep wells, which the future traveler will enjoy. Without a guide who had traversed them, we have ventured into trackless table-lands where water was not found for several marches. With crowbar and pick and axe in hand, we have worked our way over mountains, which seemed to defy aught save the wild goat, and hewed a passage through a chasm of living rock more narrow than our wagons. To bring these first wagons to the Pacific, we have preserved the strength of our mules by herding them over large tracts, which you have laboriously guarded without loss. The garrison of four presidios of Sonora concentrated within the walls of Tucson, gave us no pause. We drove them out, with their artillery, but our intercourse with the citizens was unmarked by a single act of injustice. Thus, marching half naked and half fed, and living upon wild animals, we have discovered and made a road of great value to our country.

Arrived at the first settlement of California, after a single day's rest, you cheerfully turned off from the route to this point of promised repose, to enter upon a campaign, and meet, as we supposed, the approach of the enemy; and this too, without even salt to season your sole subsistence of fiesh meat.

Lieutenant A. J. Smith and George Stoneman, of the First Dragoons, have shared and given valuable aid in all these labors.

Thus, volunteers, you have exhibited some high and essential qualities of veterans. But much remains undone. Soon, you will turn your attention to the drill, to system and order, to forms also, which are all necessary to the soldier."

By order, etc.

IV.

CALIFORNIA.

UPPER California was discovered by Cabrillo, a Spanish navigator, A. D. 1548. It was first colonized in 1768.

Presidios, or garrisoned forts, were established at San Diego, first, at Santa Barbara, Monterey, San Francisco; the form of all of them is nearly the same; adobe walls twelve feet high, enclosing a square of six hundred feet fronts, and including a chapel and store houses; they were weak, but sufficient for defence against wild Indians, whom they called gentiles; the garrisons were of about eighty horsemen, some auxiliaries, and small detachments of artillery.

Missions of Franciscans accompanied, or immediately followed them, at San Diego first; from time to time above twenty more. There was one near each presidio, walled like them. They included handsome churches, some of stone, ample quarters, work shops, store houses, granaries and courts. They gradually extended their claims to territory, and so came to include nearly the whole country. The conversion of natives went hand in hand with their instruction in agriculture and mechanical arts, and the use of the Spanish language; they were the laborers in the erection of those great structures. Their villages, called rancherias, were near the missions; they lived in thatched conical huts. Small military detachments were quartered at the rancherias to keep order. In 1822 the number of the converts was estimated at twenty-two thousand, besides gentiles settled near by.

There was some immigration from Mexico; the soldiers generally brought wives, and thus the white population was slowly increased. The white race, living an active out-door life, in a most genial climate, was healthy and strong, and of extreme fecundity; the presidial companies came to be composed of them; but it was difficult for them to secure the ownership of land, against the encroachments of the powerful missions, which discouraged immigration, and under an irregular and weak territorial government, the head of which was the commandantegeneral. Thus their state was not far above savagery; there were no schools; a little wheat, beans, etc., was raised by families; their diet was chiefly fresh meat; even milk was seldom used, and butter almost unknown. They were indolent although active; almost lived on horseback, and were wonderful riders; they and the Comanches more nearly realizing the fabled centaurs than any people known to us. Horse-racing, gambling, and dancing were their chief occupations. Still they had received from the poor Indians the designation of people of reason (*jente de razon*).

The cattle and horses introduced—the latter said to be of Arabian breed—wonderfully increased on the rich grasses in a most favorable climate. Up to 1826, horses which had become wholly wild, so overran the land, that it was common for the men to join together to drive them into great pens, prepared for the purpose, and when thus confined, after securing some of the finest animals, to slaughter the rest.

In 1816 a foreign trade in hides and tallow was opened; an annual ship came from Boston; in 1822 near forty thousand hides and about the same number of arrobas (twenty-five pounds) of tallow were exported. Hides became known as California bank notes, of the value of two dollars.

The Spanish power in California was overthrown by the Mexican revolution of 1822; and the policy of the ever-changing governments of Mexico showed itself constant in the secularization of the government of California. The Missions began to decline in wealth and power in 1824. The decree for the expulsion of all native Spaniards was enforced on their priests; and by 1836 the Fathers were finally stripped of their possessions.

It was a sad change for the Indians, who were strongly attached to their spiritual guides and governors, and were happy and content under their jurisdiction. The Missions gradually despoiled,— the Californians taking an active part—under secular administration, the proselytes became scattered or subject to every oppression and cruelty,— mere serfs.

But this wrong and devastation had compensating effects upon the people at large. The lands became divided, and came into individual ownership; industry and enterprise were encouraged in those who were no longer dependent upon the bounty and the will of priests.

In the spring of 1846 the white population of California was, by estimate, no higher than ten thousand; including about two thousand foreigners chiefly from the United States. These last beginning to arrive so rapidly, their superior intelligence and energy had aroused the jealousy of prominent natives.

The year before there had been (no uncommon thing) a revolution headed by natives,—Castro, Alvarado and Pio Pico, in which foreigners took part—which resulted in the expulsion of General Micheltorena, the Mexican governor.

General Castro assumed command of the military, and soon after issued a proclamation, understood to require all Americans to leave the country. But no immediate measures were taken to enforce the order, and it was disregarded by the immigrants.

In the winter of 1845-6, Brevet Captain Fremont, topographical engineers, under favor of a roving commission of explorations, by extraordinary coincidence, made his appearance at the head of sixty or seventy well armed adventurers, in government pay, among the northern settlements; and he obtained permission from Castro to remain, for the purpose of refreshing his men and horses. Rumors of a change and of an intended attack by Castro, reached him; whereupon he fortified himself in the mountains which overlook Monterey. But after remaining a few days, he determined, early in the month of March, to proceed to Oregon, and before the middle of May he had reached Lake Klamath in Oregon.

Suddenly he was overtaken in that mountain wilderness by a messenger from Washington city. It was Lieutenant Gillespie, of the United States Marine Corps. Captain Fremont turned with his "surveying" party to retrace his journey.

This remarkable occurrence has its explanation. Senator Thomas H. Benton with the foresight of a statesman, aspiring to be, if not actually, the controlling influence of President Polk's administration, was tempted by paternal ambition to anticipate legal war, and used his influence to have sent, long before its occurrence, a messenger to California, where, he must have had reason to believe, Captain Fremont would be found; he bore a communication to Fremont urging, of course, his great opportunity as the head of seventy veteran woodsmen and the hardy immigrants in Northern California to forestal the war and revolutionize the country, or, at the least, to be present and ready to reap the first fruits of the war.* Lieutenant Gillespie, an officer of fine address, who spoke perfectly the language of Mexico, was selected and sent through that country, then the speediest route. Arrived at Monterey, with a dispatch for our consul there—probably to require his assistance—he found that Captain Fremont, seemingly with no taste for the commotions already begun, and the threatened attack of Castro, had abandoned to the Mexican revolutionist the field of a great opportunity. Then Gillespie's true mission was developed, and he proceeded at great risks to follow his trail, until he overtook him and delivered instructions which he could not fail to heed.

About the 1st of June the lieutenant commanding the Mexican garrison of Sonoma was ordered to remove a drove of government horses from the mission of San Rafael to Santa Clara, General Castro's headquarters. To accomplish this, the

* Early in the war Colonel Benton was nearly successful in an intrigue to be appointed a Lieutenant-General, to supersede Winfield Scott.

officer and small party crossed the Sacramento at Sutter's Fort, New Helvetia, the nearest point at which the horses could swim the river. An Indian, having seen the movement, reported among the American settlers that two or three hundred armed men were advancing up the Sacramento Valley.

The alarm was spread through the valley by swift messengers; and most of the immigrants joined Captain Fremont, who by this time was sixty or seventy miles above Sutter's Fort.

The truth with regard to the lieutenant's party was soon known, with the addition, true or not, that the object of the slight affair was to mount a force to march against the Americans.

After consultation it was resolved that the California party should be pursued, as the capture of the horses would weaken Castro, and for a time frustrate his designs. Twelve men volunteered and chose a Mr. Merritt for their leader. They followed and surprised the party June the 10th, when it surrendered, without resistance, the horses and their arms. They were given each a horse to ride, and were released. The "Bear" revolution was now fairly begun, and the only safety lay in its vigorous prosecution. The same party, increased to above thirty, marched directly upon Sonoma, and on June 14th, took possession without resistance of the town and military post; they found there nine pieces of artillery and two hundred stand of small arms. Several officers of high rank were captured, but with much consideration and politeness on both sides, General Vallejo, one of them, sent for his caballada and remounted the whole party. Private property was scrupulously respected.

A small garrison was left in Sonoma, and was soon increased to forty men under command of William B. Ide.

June 18th, his garrison assenting, Mr. Ide, filled with the spirit of '76, and infected by the grandiloquent style of the people of the land which they wished to adopt as their own, issued a proclamation; General Castro had issued two, the day before.

> A proclamation to all persons and citizens of the district of Sonoma, requesting them to remain at peace, and follow their rightful occupations without fear of molestation.
> The Commander-in-chief of the troops assembled at the fortress of Sonoma, gives his inviolable pledge to all persons in California, not found under arms, that they shall not be disturbed in their persons, their property, or social relations, one with another, by men under his command.
> He also solemnly declares his object to be, to defend himself and companions in arms, who were invited to this country

by a promise of lands on which to settle themselves and families; who were also promised a Republican government; when having arrived in California, they were denied the privilege of buying or renting lands of their friends; who, instead of being allowed to participate in, or being protected by a Republican government, were oppressed by a military despotism; who were even threatened by proclamation, by the chief officers of the aforesaid despotism, with extermination if they should not depart out of the country, leaving all their property, arms, and beasts of burden; and thus deprived of their means of flight or defence, we were to be driven through deserts inhabited by hostile Indians, to certain destruction.

To overthrow a government which has seized upon the property of the Missions for its individual aggrandizement; which has ruined and shamefully oppressed the laboring people of California, by their enormous exactions on goods imported into the country,—is the determined purpose of the brave men who are associated under my command.

I also solemnly declare my object, in the second place, to be to invite all peaceable and good citizens of California, who are friendly to the maintenance of good order and equal rights, and I do hereby invite them to repair to my camp at Sonoma, without delay, to assist in establishing and perpetuating a Republican Government, which shall secure to all, civil and religious liberty; which shall encourage virtue and literature; which shall leave unshackled by fetters, agriculture, commerce, and manufactures.

I further declare that I rely upon the rectitude of our intentions, the favor of Heaven, and the bravery of those who are bound and associated with me, by the principles of self-preservation, by the love of truth, and the hatred of tyranny, for my hopes of success.

I furthermore declare, that I believe that a government to be prosperous and happy, must originate with a people who are friendly to its existence; that the citizens are its guardians, the officers its servants, its glory its reward.

  (Signed)   WILLIAM B. IDE.
Headquarters, Sonoma, June 18th, 1846.

General Castro's two short proclamations, issued practically at the same time, were moderate for a Mexican, and should be considered in any view of the merits of the situation.

The citizen Jose Castro, lieutenant-colonel of cavalry in the Mexican army, and acting general-commander of the department of California.

Fellow Citizens:—The contemptible policy of the agents of the United States of North America, in this department, has induced a portion of adventurers, who, regardless of the rights of men, have daringly commenced an invasion, possessing themselves of the town of Sonoma, taking by surprise at that place, the military commander of that border, Colonel Don Mariano Guadalupe Valléjo, Lieut.-colonel Don Victor Prudon, Captain Don Salvador Valléjo, and Mr. Jacob P. Leese.

Fellow Countrymen:—The defence of our liberty, the true religion which our fathers possessed, and our independence, calls upon us to sacrifice ourselves, rather than lose these inestimable blessings; banish from your hearts all petty resentments, turn you, and behold yourselves, these families, these innocent little ones, which have unfortunately fallen into the hands of our enemies, dragged from the bosoms of their fathers, who are prisoners among foreigners, and are calling upon us to succor them. There is still time for us to rise "en masse" as irresistible as retributive. You need not doubt but Divine Providence will direct us in the way to glory. You should not vacillate because of the smallness of the garrison of the general headquarters, for he who first will sacrifice himself will be your friend and fellow citizen.   JOSE CASTRO.

Headquarters, Santa Clara, June 17th, 1846.

Citizen Jose Castro, lieutenant-colonel of artillery in the Mexican army, and acting general-commander of the department of Upper California.

All foreigners residing among us, occupied with their business, may rest assured of the protection of all the authorities of the department, while they refrain entirely from all revolutionary movements.

The general commandancia under my charge will never proceed with rigor against any persons, neither will its authority result in mere words, wanting proof to support it; declaration shall be taken, proofs executed, and the liberty and rights of the laborious, which is ever commendable, shall be protected.

Let the fortune of war take its chance with those ungrateful men, who, with arms in their hands, have attacked the country, without recollecting they were treated by the undersigned with all the indulgence of which he is so characteristic. The inhabitants of the department are witnesses to the truth of this. I have nothing to fear, my duty leads me to death or victory. I am a Mexican soldier, and I will be free and independent, or I will gladly die for these inestimable blessings.

JOSE CASTRO.

Headquarters, Santa Clara, June 17th, 1846.

About this time, two young men, T. Corvie and Fowler, were captured in the neighborhood of Sonoma by one Padilla. They were taken to his camp, and, a day or two after, were cruelly tortured to death.*

Their disappearance was soon known, and their murder suspected; and the commander of Sonoma hearing of several prisoners in Padilla's camp, sent Captain Ford and twenty-one men to attack him, at his supposed position at Santa Rosa plains. Arrived

---

* "What I saw in California," by E. Bryant, afterward captain of Fremont's battalion, and Alcalde of San Francisco.

there, it was found that Captain De la Torre had joined Padilla with seventy men, and that they had gone in the direction of San Rafael. Marching all night, Ford, having ridden sixty miles, surprised the enemy, taking breakfast, twelve miles from San Rafael; they were in a house about sixty yards from a clump of brushwood. Dismounting there, Captain Ford, ordering that not a shot should be wasted, advanced upon the house. After a short resistance, a sergeant and party charging upon the Americans, the Californians took to flight, leaving eight killed and two wounded. They rallied on a hill, about a mile off; but showing no disposition to return, Captain Ford exchanged his tired horses for fresh ones, found there in a corral, and rode back to Sonoma.

"Captain Fremont, having heard that Don Jose Castro was crossing the bay with two hundred men, marched and joined the garrison of Sonoma, on the 25th of June. Several days were spent in active pursuit of the party under Captain De la Torre, but they succeeded in crossing the bay before they could be overtaken. With the retreat of De la

Torre ended all opposition on the north side of the Bay of San Francisco."*

Captain Fremont, then, with about one hundred and seventy men, returned to the mouth of the American River near Sutter's Fort.

A small party under R. Semple was ordered to cross the Bay, to the town of San Francisco, then called Yerba Buena, to seize the captain of the port, R. T. Ridley; which was done, and Ridley was taken to New Helvetia, (Sutter's Fort,) July 8th; there other prisoners were in confinement.

Commodore Sloat, in the United States Frigate *Savannah*, arrived at Monterey on the second of July; he had heard of a collision in arms upon the Rio Grande, but not of the declaration of Congress that war existed. But on the 7th, he determined to hoist the American flag in Monterey, and it was done by Captain Mervine with two hundred and fifty seamen and marines, amid cheers of troops and foreigners, and with a salute from each of the ships in the harbor. At the same time a proclamation was read, and posted in the town, both in English and Spanish.

* " What I saw in California." p. 293.

In it he announced that the two nations being actually at war, he should carry the flag throughout California; he came as the best friend of the inhabitants as "henceforth California will be a portion of the United States." Judges and alcaldes were invited to continue to execute the functions of their offices; and supplies and provisions should be promptly paid for at fair rates. Under instructions from Commodore Sloat, Captain Montgomery, of the *Portsmouth,* which lay at San Francisco, landed seventy sailors and marines and hoisted the United States flag in the public square; and a volunteer company of Americans was immediately organized for the defence of the town. On the 10th, a national flag was sent by Captain Montgomery to Sonoma; the Bear flag was lowered, and the American flag was raised amid the shouts of the garrison.

Purser Fauntleroy, of the *Savannah* at Monterey, had been ordered to organize a mounted company, from the ships and citizens, in order to keep up communication with the northern posts held by immigrants; it marched July 17th, to take possession of the Mission of San Juan, about thirty miles east of

Monterey. Captain Fremont, having left his position on the Sacramento River on the 12th, arrived at San Juan about an hour before him, and occupied the Mission without opposition. Nine pieces of cannon, two hundred old muskets and a store of ammunition were found there. Both parties marched to Monterey next day.

At every important point in northern California the American flag was now flying.

Fortifications at Monterey were begun immediately after its occupation. Commodore R. F. Stockton arrived there July 15th, in the frigate *Congress*, and on the 23d Commodore Sloat sailed in the *Levant* for Panama.

General Castro retreating, had joined Governor Pio Pico at Santa Barbara, when the joint forces numbered about six hundred; they then marched for Los Angeles and arrived there early in August.

Immediately after taking command, Commodore Stockton sailed in the Congress, July 25th, for San Pedro, the port of Los Angeles, and at the same time sent the *Cyane*, Captain Dupont, with Captain Fremont and volunteers on board, to San Diego. The frigate *Savannah* remained at Monterey, and the sloop Portsmouth at San Francisco.

Arrived at San Pedro, twenty-five miles south of Los Angeles, Commodore Stockton landed a large force of sailors and marines from the Congress, and marched for Los Angeles, his artillery being dragged by oxen. At his approach to the camp of the Californians, close to the town, they fled without resistance; and the capital was occupied without opposition on the 12th of August. The Californians dispersed, and General Castro with a few followers took the road to Sonora.

Captain Fremont had previously been landed at San Diego, about one hundred and forty miles south of Los Angeles, and met with difficulty in procuring horses; he marched to Los Angeles with eighty men, and arrived several days after Castro's flight.*

Commodore Stockton, on the 17th of August, issued a proclamation as "Commander-in-chief, and Governor of California." It announced that the "Territory of California now belongs to the United States," and the people were "requested to meet in their several towns and departments, at such time

* What I saw in California, p. 297.

and place as they may see fit, to elect civil officers to fill the places of those who decline to continue in office, and to administer the laws according to the former usages of the territory."

Thorough protection in "liberty of conscience," persons and property was promised.

"The California battalion of mounted riflemen will be kept in the service of the territory, and constantly on duty, to prevent and punish any aggressions by the Indians, or any other persons, upon the property of individuals, or the peace of the territory; and California hereafter shall be so governed and defended as to give security to the inhabitants, and to defy the power of Mexico.

"All persons are required, as long as the territory is under martial law, to be in their houses from ten o'clock at night until sunrise in the morning."

On the 22d he issued a proclamation for the election of alcaldes to take place September 22d, and soon after another without date, announcing a territorial form of government.

In an official letter, dated August 27th, to "Major Fremont, California battalion," he authorized him to increase the battalion to three hundred men, and to garrison the five principal towns, and informed him that before he left the territory, it was his intention to appoint him "governor, and Captain Gillespie the secretary thereof."

Captain Gillespie was left in command at Los Angeles; fifty men had been ordered to constitute the garrison.

On the 27th of September, about a month later, the frigate *Congress*, Captain Livingston, bearing the broad pennant of Commodore Stockton, and the frigate *Savannah*, Captain Mervine, anchored in the harbor of San Francisco, having sailed from Monterey a day or two before.

October 1st, a courier arrived from the south with news of an insurrection of the Californians, which occurred September 23d at Los Angeles, and of the capture by them of an American merchantvessel lying at San Pedro. The *Savannah* immediately sailed for San Pedro.

At this time there were in the harbor of San Francisco, vessels of many nations, and among them a ship of the French navy, and a Russian brig from Sitka, commanded by a naval officer, and laden with wheat.

Commodore Stockton having given two days' notice, landed October 5th, being received with a great parade, naval, marine and civil, with music and speeches; rode out to the mission of San Francisca Dolores, to a collation at the house of Captain Leidesdorff,—at which he spoke an hour—returning to a ball in town that night.

Major Fremont, who had returned to the north to recruit his battalion, having arrived from the Sacramento with his volunteers, on the 12th, the next day Commodore Stockton in the Congress, and Fremont's one hundred and eighty volunteers in a transport, sailed for the south—San Pedro or San Diego, it was understood.

Meantime Captain Mervine, having arrived at San Pedro, landed about four hundred of the sailors and marines of the *Savannah*, and marched for Los Angeles; being met on the Mesa by a large force of insurgents, he was defeated, losing six men killed, and retreated to his ship. Captain Gillespie surrendered Los Angeles. Santa Barbara was beleaguered, but Lieutenant Talbot, with his garrison of twenty-five men, forced his way out, and after suffering many hardships, reached Monterey in safety.

Commodore Stockton had now one hundred and eighty volúnteers added to the force with which he had before captured Los Angeles; but doubtless hearing of Captain Mervine's defeat, entered the harbor of Monterey about the 24th of October, after being *about twelve days at sea*, and landed Major Fremont and his volunteers in order that the battalion should be recruited, and organized on a larger scale.

From this time until January, 1847, when General Kearny had arrived, the Californians were in little disturbed possession of the country, save the three ports,—San Francisco, Monterey and San Diego.

Major Fremont was taking measures to collect volunteers, and to mount the battalion, in order to march to the south. November 15th, Mr. T. O. Larkin, U. S. Consul at Monterey, was captured and maltreated by a large force of Californians, about twenty miles north of that town; who also the same day attacked a party of Americans who were driving four hundred horses to Major Fremont's camp at Monterey, killing and wounding six of the party; but eight others took refuge in a grove, and defended themselves for an hour, against one hundred and thirty Californians; when, being joined by a party of fifty immigrant volunteers, the insurgents gradually drew off.

However, they still kept rallying, and firing now and then a musket at the Americans, until eleven o'clock at night, when "one of the Walla-Walla Indians offered his services to come into Monterey and give Colonel Fremont notice of what was passing. Soon after he started he was pursued by a party of the enemy. The foremost in pursuit drove a lance at the Indian, who, trying to parry it, received the lance through his hand; he immediately, with the other hand, seized his tomahawk, and struck a blow at his opponent, which split his head from the crown to the mouth. By this time the others had come up, and with the most extraordinary dexterity and bravery, the Indian vanquished two more, and the rest ran away. He rode on towards this town as far as his horse was able to carry him, and came in on foot."*

Major Fremont marched from Monterey as soon as he heard of this skirmish, but did not meet with the Californians; he then camped at the Mission of

---

* "Californian" newspaper, Monterey, Nov. 21st.

San Juan, waiting the arrival of volunteers from the north.

He marched ten miles south, Nov. 28th, and in camp there the reorganization of the battalion was completed. It consisted of four hundred and twenty-eight men, including a few Indians, and was divided into eight companies of mounted men, with three officers to each; officers and privates were armed with rifle and holster pistols; besides a bowie knife and in some cases a brace of pistols in waist belts. Attached were two pieces of artillery, under command of Louis McLane and John K. Wilson, both of the navy.

Besides mules for packing baggage, five or six hundred horses, for remounts, were driven with the battalion.

The battalion marched ten miles November 30th; finding no cattle in the vicinity of the camp, a party was sent back to the Mission, who returned with one hundred head. These were driven for future use.

There was much rain, and the grass was young and tender; these causes together produced constant failure and exhaustion in the horses. The march was resumed December 3d; and eleven days averaged eleven miles a day. Other rations exhausted, the battalion consumed an average of ten pounds a day of fat beef.*

The Mission San Miguel, on the heads of the Salinas River, was passed December 10th. " Under the administration of the *padres* it was a wealthy establishment, and manufactures of various kinds were carried on. They raised immense numbers of sheep, the fleeces of which were manufactured by the Indians into blankets and coarse cloths. Their granaries were filled with an abundance of maize and frijoles, and their store rooms with other necessaries of life from the ranchos belonging to the mission lands in the vicinity. Now all the buildings, except the church and principal range of houses contiguous, have fallen into ruins, and an Englishman, his wife and one child, with two or three Indian servants, are the sole inhabitants. The church is the largest I have seen in the country, and its interior is in good repair. . . The Englishman professes to have purchased the mission and all the lands belonging to it for $300." *

" *December* 12*th*.—To relieve our horses, which

---

* "What I saw in California."

are constantly giving out, the entire battalion were ordered to march on foot, turning their horses with the saddles and bridles upon them, into the general *caballada*, to be driven along by the horse guard. An Indian, said to be the servant of Tortorio Pico, was captured here by the advance party. A letter was found upon him, but its contents I never learned."

December 13*th*.—" Mr. Stanley, one of the volunteers, and one of the gentlemen who so kindly supplied us with provisions on Mary's River, died last night. . . He was buried this morning, . . and the ashes of a braver or a better man will never repose in the lonely hills of California."

After the funeral the battalion was marched a short distance to witness another scene. The Indian captured at the rancho yesterday was condemned to die. He was tied to a tree. Here he stood some fifteen or twenty minutes, until the Indians from a neighboring rancheria could be brought to witness the execution. A file of soldiers was then ordered to fire upon him. He fell upon his knees and remained in that position several minutes without uttering a groan, and then sank upon the earth. No human being could have met his fate with more composure, or with stronger manifestations of courage. It was a scene such as I desire never to witness again.*

Next day the battalion reached the mission of San Luis Obispo, and remained there two rainy days.

A party was sent, and captured Tortorio Pico, a conspicuous revolutionist. On the 16th he was brought before a court martial, and tried for forfeiture of parole and sentenced to death.

December 17th.—"While standing in one of the corridors this morning, a procession of females passed by me, headed by a lady of fine appearance and dressed with remarkable taste and neatness, compared with those who followed her. Their *rebosos* concealed the faces of most of them, except the leader, whose beautiful features, I dare say, she thought (and justly) required no concealment. They proceeded to the quarters of Colonel Fremont and their object . . . was to petition for the . . . pardon of Pico . . . whose execution was expected to take place this morning. Their intercession was

* "What I saw in California."

successful, as no execution took place, and in a short time all the prisoners were discharged."*

December 24th, the battalion ascended the St. Inez Mountains, and there camped. There, they overlooked the beautiful plain of Santa Barbara. " With the spy glass, we could see in the plain far below us, herds of cattle quietly grazing upon the green herbage which carpets its gentle undulations. The plain is dotted with groves, surrounding the springs and belting the small water-courses, of which there were many flowing from this range of mountains. Ranchos are scattered far up and down the plain, but not one human being could be seen stirring. About ten or twelve miles to the south, the white towers of the Mission Santa Barbara raise themselves. Beyond is the illimitable waste of waters." † On the mountain the shrubbery was in bloom.

But next day, Christmas, came a great rain storm, and the three miles of descent was scarcely

---

* Being an officer of the battalion, Mr. Bryant makes no comment upon the different fates of the principal, and his ignorant tool, the brave Indian, who had no beautiful friend. And yet irrespective of the question of the criminality of the Indian, would it not be impossible to discover any sanction or human authority for his trial

† "What I saw in California."

accomplished, even in the night following; the cannon and some baggage were left,—to be sent for next day,—and about one hundred horses lost their lives (the loss in the month had been about seven hundred).

December 27th, they camped a half mile from Santa Barbara. About a hundred miles to the south the final battles were impending; they were fought about two weeks later. Californians visited the camp, and the prize schooner *Julia* came into port, and landed a piece of artillery for the battalion. But the battalion lay at Santa Barbara a week.

New Years day was celebrated by the Indians of the mission and town by a procession, music, etc. They marched through the streets of the deserted town to the tune of Yankee Doodle.

The weather for that week was the April of the Middle Atlantic States; the thermometer ranged from fifty to seventy degrees.

The battalion marched ten miles January 3d, 1847. Next night, after a march of six miles they

for a capital offence, and his execution by this "battalion" of volunteers, who did not have a single commission or legal appointment among them?

10*

camped on the beach in the Rincon, where they apprehended opposition; but the *Julia* lay in sight to cover the passage; and on the 5th they reached the mission of San Buenaventure, and camped at two o'clock. Soon after a small party of Californians were seen on a hill; the battalion was called to arms, the cannon were fired, and " they scampered away like a flock of antelopes."

Only a few Indians were found at the mission; the white population had abandoned it at the approach of the battalion.

January 6th, having marched six or seven miles, a party of sixty or seventy mounted Californians showed themselves in front; a Delaware and a California Indian in advance beckoned and shouted to the battalion to come on, but in vain; it was turned into, and followed far, a cañon, until it was impracticable for the artillery to follow; it had to retrace its ascent;* the Californians were prancing and waving banners and arms; but the two brave Indians rode towards them, and exchanged some shots, when the Californians soon disappeared. The battalion went into camp.

*" What I saw in California."

This California detachment, having accomplished their probable object, no doubt returned to take part in the battles of January 8th and 9th.

Next day the battalion again marched but seven miles.

On the 8th, twelve miles were marched; horses and men had lately fared well; forage, beans and vegetables having become plentiful. Besides the regular guard, one-fourth of the battalion were kept under arms during the night.

Next morning early, Captain Hamley arrived in camp with dispatches from Commodore Stockton: he had landed at Santa Barbara, and followed the battalion. The battalion marched twelve miles.

On the 10th, a few Californians, supposed to be the same who had stopped the march on the 6th, showed themselves, having had time to return from the battles of the Mesa of Los Angeles. The battalion camped, having marched ten miles.

On the 11th of January it took quarters at the mission of San Fernando, at 1 o'clock P. M.

There were found thousands of bushels of corn, noble gardens, roses in bloom, oranges, lemons, figs, olives in full bearing, large herds of cattle and sheep grazing on the luxuriant plain.

Having followed, to its last ominous pause, the slow* march of this battalion, (which had little or no effect upon the enemy or the war, and resulted in unprecedented official demoralization, but fortunately in no other serious injury to the public service) let them be left in such good quarters, while the reader turns to trace the fortunes,—until they culminate in peace and order to California—of that veteran and proved public servant, General Kearny. He was left deceived as to the subjugation of California, and entering, with only an escort, the unknown mountains of the Gila River.

General Kearny's March to the Pacific.

General Kearny was left turning westward from the Rio Grande, October 15th, 1846; among his staff were Captain H. S. Turner, First Dragoons, Lieutenant W. H. Emory, Topographical Engineers, and Captain A. R. Johnston, First Dragoons A. D. C.; his escort was 100 men of First Dragoons commanded by Captain Ben. Moore and Lieutenant T. C. Hammond, and mounted on mules; also two

* Three hundred and fifty miles in forty-three days.

mountain howitzers in charge of Lieut. J. W. Davidson, First Dragoons. The baggage was packed on mules.

They first passed over high plains, intersected by several bold streams; their richness and admirable fitness for grazing are extolled. On the 18th they reached the old copper mines on the second branch of the Mimbres. "They are said to be very rich, both in copper and gold, and the specimens obtained maintain this assertion. We learn that those who worked them made their fortunes; but the Apaches did not like their proximity, and one day turned out and destroyed the mining town, driving off the inhabitants. There are remains of twenty or thirty adobe houses, and ten or fifteen shafts sinking into the earth." *

October 19*th*.—The country passed over in the first part of the day was beautiful; it was a succession of high, rolling hills.

Thirteen miles from the copper mines was passed the sulphur spring of San Lucia, in a beautiful valley, and that night camp was made after dark on Night Creek, the mire of which was very disturb-

* " Notes of a military reconnoissance, by Lieutenant-Colonel W. H. Emory."

ing under the circumstances. Here had been appointed a meeting with Apaches, for the purpose of trade for mules. They came early, headed by Red Sleeve. He said "the road was opened forever, one white man could pass in safety." The trade was a failure, the Indians being extravagant in their demands. "At length the call of 'boots and saddles' was sounded. The order, quickness and quietude of our movements seemed to impress them. One of the chiefs, after eying the General with great apparent admiration, broke out in a vehement manner, 'you have taken New Mexico, and will soon take California, go then and take Chihuahua, Durango and Sonora. We will help you. You fight for land, we care nothing for land; we fight for the laws of Montezuma and for food. The Mexicans are rascals, we hate and will kill them all.' There burst out the smothered fire of three hundred years! Finding we were more indifferent than they supposed to trade, . . . they became at once eager for traffic . . . My packs were made. One of the gentlest mules at that moment took fright, and went off like a rocket, on the back trail, scattering to the right and left all who opposed him. A large, elegant looking woman, mounted a-straddle, more valiant than the rest, faced the brute and charged upon him at full speed. This turned his course back to camp, and I rewarded her with half-a dozen biscuits, and through her intervention, succeeded in trading two broken-down mules for two good ones, giving two yards of scarlet cloth in the bargain. By this time a large number of Indians had collected about us, all differently dressed, and some in the most fantastical style. The Mexican dress and saddles predominated, showing where they had chiefly made up their wardrobe. One had a jacket made of a Henry Clay flag, which aroused unpleasant sensations, for the acquisition no doubt cost one of our countrymen his life. Several wore beautiful helmets, decked with black feathers, which with the short shirt, waist belt, bare legs and buskins, gave them the look of pictures of antique Grecian warriors. Most were furnished with the Mexican cartridge box. . . . . .

"These men have no fixed homes. Their houses are of twigs, made easily and deserted with indifference. They hover around the beautiful hills that overhang the Del Norte, between the 31st and 32d parallels of latitude, and look down upon the states of Chihuahua and Sonora, and woe to the luckless company that ventures out unguarded by a strong force. Their hills are covered with luxuriant grama, which enables them to keep their horses in fine order, so that they can always pursue with rapidity and return in safety. . . . We wended our way through the narrow valley of Night Creek. On each side were huge stone buttes shooting up into the skies. At one place we were compelled to mount one of these spurs, almost perpendicular . . . a pack slipped from a mule, and although not shaped favorably for the purpose, rolled entirely to the bottom of the hill, up which the mules had climbed."*

October 21st was a bad day, the steep ascents and descents causing the packs to cut the animals' backs; the howitzers did not reach camp; one of them, in the dark, with its mule, rolled down into a steep ravine, but without injury.

October 23d, they passed one of the famous ruins; but the only evidences of handicraft remaining were immense quantities of broken pottery, extending for two miles along the river.

* Notes of a Military Reconnoissance.

Deer and beaver, the blue quail, teal, etc., were found on the Upper Gila.

October 25*th*.—" We were now in the regions made famous in olden times, by the fables of Friar Marcos, and eagerly did we ascend every mound, expecting to see in the distance what I fear is but the fabulous 'Casa Montezuma.' Once, as we turned a sharp hill, the bold outline of a castle presented itself, with the tops of the walls horizontal, the corners vertical, and apparently one front bastioned. My companion agreed with me that at last we beheld this famous building; restless for the show, I drew out my telescope, when to my disappointment a clay butte, with regular horizontal seams, stood in the place of our castle; but to the naked eye the delusion was complete. The Indians here do not know the name Aztec; Montezuma is the outward point in their chronology,—a name at this moment as familiar to every Indian, Pueblo, Apache and Navajo, as that of our Savior or Washington is to us. In the person of Montezuma they unite both qualities of divinity and patriot.

" We passed to-day the ruins of two more villages similar to those of yesterday. The foundation of the largest house seen yesterday was sixty by twenty feet; to-day, forty by thirty; the stone forming the supposed foundations was round and unhewn; and some cedar logs were also found about the houses, much decayed, bearing no mark of an edged tool."*

A cactus, first seen there, but common further south, was well described as "eighteen inches high, and eighteen inches in its greatest diameter, containing twenty vertical volutes, armed with strong spines." They contain much water.

The next day was very severe upon the party; they were eight and a half hours passing over a rough mountain, several thousand feet above the river; they named it "Devil's turnpike;" twelve or fifteen mules were lost. Opposite this day's journey, three small rivers enter the Gila, through cañons; they are called the Black, the Blue, and the St. Charles. The howitzers got to camp in the afternoon of the next day. (These weigh only two hundred pounds; the wheels are three feet apart, and about three feet four inches in diameter.)

Next day, soon clear of the mountain, there was a march of twenty miles along the Gila valley,

* Notes of a Military Reconnoisance.

and the night camp was opposite Mount Graham. Along almost the whole distance were found the remains of houses such as before mentioned; traces of circular enclosures of four hundred yards in diameter; the foundations of houses from twenty to one hundred feet front; but no marks of edged tools, no utensils except the remains of pottery of immense amount, and the rude corn-grinder used by the Indians of to-day. "I do not think it improbable that these ruins may be those of comparatively modern Indians, for Vanegas says, 'The Father, Jacob Sedelmayer, in October, 1744, set out from his mission, (Tubutuma) and, after travelling eighty leagues, reached the Gila, where he found six thousand Papagos, and near the same number of Pimos and Maricopas;' and the map which he gives of this country, although very incorrect, represents many Indian settlements and missions on the river. His observations, however, were confined to that part of the Gila River near its mouth." *

October 29th, they marched twenty-one miles in the Gila bottom grounds; the whole plain, from three to six miles wide, within reach of irrigation; and

* Notes of a Military Reconnoissance.

the scarce and crisp vegetation and plenteous pottery indicated that irrigation must have been used. " The crimson tinted Sierra Carlos skirted the river on the north side the whole day, and its changing profiles formed subjects of study and amusement. Sometimes we could trace a Gothic steeple ; then a horse ; now an old woman's face, and again a veritable steamboat ; but this required the assistance of a light smoky cloud, drifting to the east, over what represented the chimney stack."

Near this camp were very large ruins, judged to have been the abode of five or ten thousand souls.

Next day a drove of the Mexican wild hogs, (peccary) found also in Texas, was chased, but without success. Several Indians appeared on a hill ; they were spoken to " but they could not be induced to come into camp; they have been dealt with by Americans in the employment of Chihuahua ; who have hunted them at fifty dollars a scalp, as we would hunt wolves ; and one American decoyed a large number of their brethren in rear of a wagon to trade, and fired a field-piece among them. It is no wonder then, that two parties of God's creatures, who never knew each other before, should meet in a desert, and not approach near enough to shake hands."*

October 31st, after a short march camp was made opposite the mouth of the San Francisco River. Carson with a party went on to explore, as in coming from California he was sixty miles without water, cut off from the river by impassable cañons. The mules were fast failing; and the appearance of three well mounted Apaches on a hill was very welcome. The Apaches could supply them. They would only suffer themselves to be approached by one person; after a long parley by signs and gestures they announced that their chief was near with mules which he would bring in ; but none came.

Next day there was no alternative, the jornada must be begun ; when the river could no longer be followed, they grazed the animals a short time on luxurious grama, filled every possible vessel with water, and commenced the ascent; but, seven miles up the hills, converging trails were observed, and they led to a fine spring, with cottonwood trees and some poor grass; there they camped, but the howitzers did not arrive.

* Journal of Captain A. R. Johnston, First Dragoons.

"That morning was first seen the *Cereus giganteus*, called in California pitahaya; it is a columnar cactus, from twenty-five to sixty feet high: some of them have no branch. Next morning, when ready for a very early start, an alarm was given, and a hill near by was seen to be lined with horsemen. They were Apaches; one called out in Spanish, that they wished to have a talk; 'one of you put down his rifle and come to us.' Londeau, my employé, immediately complied; I followed; but before marching half way up the steep hill, the Indian espied in my jacket the handle of a large horse pistol. He told me I must put down my pistol before he would meet me. I threw it aside and proceeded to the top of the hill, where, although he was mounted and surrounded by six or eight of his own men, armed with rifles and arrows, he received me with great agitation. The talk was long and tedious. I exhausted every argument to induce him to come into camp. His principal fear seemed to be the howitzers, which recalled at once to my mind the story I had heard of the massacre by Johnson. At last a bold young fellow, tired of the parley, threw down his rifle, and with a step which Forrest in Metamora might have envied, strode off towards camp, piloted by Carson. We were about to follow, when the chief informed us it would be more agreeable to him if we remained until his warrior returned.

"The ice was now broken, most of them seeing that their comrade encountered no danger, followed one by one. They said they belonged to the tribe of Piñon Lanos; that 'they were simple in head, but true of heart.' Presents were distributed; they promised a guide to a spring six miles distant, over the mountain, where they engaged to meet us next day with one hundred mules." *

They accordingly followed the guide to a good camp in a grove of sycamore, with a little water there rising, and sinking within one hundred yards.

November 3d, the General was again disappointed; the Indians came, but only seven mules were obtained in the whole day.

"Our visitors to-day presented the same motley group we have always found the Apaches. Among them was a middle-aged woman, whose garrulity and interference in every trade was the annoyance

* Notes of a Military Reconnoissance.

of Major Swords, who had charge of the trading, but the amusement of the bystanders.

She had on a gauze-like dress, trimmed with the richest and most costly Brussels lace, pillaged, no doubt, from some fandango-going belle of Sonora; she straddled a fine grey horse, and whenever her blanket dropped from her shoulders, her tawny form could be seen through the transparent gauze. After she had sold her mule, she was anxious to sell her horse, and careered about to show his qualities. At one time she charged at full speed up a steep hill. In this, the fastenings of her dress broke and her bare back was exposed to the crowd, who ungallantly raised a shout of laughter. Nothing daunted, she wheeled short round, with surprising dexterity, and seeing the mischief done, coolly slipped the dress from her arms and tucked it between her seat and the saddle. In this state of nudity, she rode through camp, until at last, attaining the object of her ambition, a soldier's red flannel shirt, she bade her adieu in that new costume.

A boy about twelve years of age, of uncommon beauty, was among our visitors. Happy, cheerful, and contented, he was consulted in every trade, and seemed an idol with the Apaches. It required little penetration to trace his origin from the same land as the gauze of the old woman. We tried to purchase him, but he said it was *long, long*, since he was captured, and that he had no desire to leave his master, who, he was certain, would not sell him for any money. All attempts were vain, and the lad seemed gratified both at the offer to purchase, and the refusal to sell." *

Next day they reached the Gila in about twenty-five miles; they passed several hollows among the hills, where were observed sycamore, oak, willow, cherry, mezquit, senna, cactus, agave, hackberry, ash, walnut, zola, cedar, pine, black gum and grape vines. They crossed large fresh trails of cattle, driven from Sonora.

The camp was so bad, that, although the howitzers had not arrived on the 5th, the march was continued some ten miles. Passing the foot of Saddle Mountain, the bed of a dry stream was followed to the San Pedro River, which was crossed and camp was made a mile from its mouth. Its valley was

* Notes of a Military Reconnoissance.

wide and covered with a dense growth of mezquit, cottonwood and willow; but the stream was found very narrow and only a foot deep,—smaller than one hundred miles above.

The bed of the dry stream they had followed, was the road of the Apache raiding parties; it was "deeply cut and turned at sharp angles, forming a zigzag like the bayoux laid by sappers in approaching a fortress, each turn of which, (and they were innumerable) formed a strong defensive position. The Apache once in possession of them is secure from pursuit or invasion from the Mexican." It was a highway leading from the plains of Santa Anna, Santa Cruz and Tucson, and distinctly marked by a fresh trail of horses, cattle and mules. "Nature had done her utmost to favor a condition of things which has enabled a savage and uncivilized tribe, armed with the bow and lance, to hold as tributary powers three fertile and once flourishing states, Chihuahua, Sonora, and Durango, peopled by a Christian race, countrymen of the immortal Cortez."

A day was passed in this camp, on the San Pedro, to wait for the howitzers, and to recruit the mules.

The miserable plight of these last gave serious doubt of the success of the expedition. They were five hundred miles from any white settlement, and with a probable dependence upon their animals for subsistence, as well as transportation.

"In the sandy arroyas . . that look as if they had been formed but a year or two since, was broken pottery, and the remains of a large building, similar in form, substance and apparent antiquity, to those so often described ; . . . my thoughts went back to the States . . . and I was struck most forcibly with the fact that not one object in the whole view, animal, vegetable, or mineral, had anything in common with the products of any State in the Union, with the single exception of the cottonwood. . . The only animals seen, were lizards, scorpions and tarantulas."

On the 7th they advanced seventeen miles in the wide bottom of the Gila. There were many geese, blue quail and turkeys ; signs of deer, beaver, and the musk hog. Three Indians were seen, and induced to enter the camp: after feasting heartily, they departed with a promise to bring mules ; but meeting the howitzers, they were so filled with astonishment, that they followed the guns to camp in mute wonder.

The next day was through a cañon of the Gila; and there was much obstruction from sand, and dense growth of willow. "Our course was traversed by a seam of yellowish colored igneous rock, shooting up into irregular spires and turrets, one or two thousand feet in height. It ran at right angles to the river, and extended to the north, and to the south, in a chain of mountains as far as the eye could reach. One of these towers was capped with a substance many hundred feet thick, disposed in horizontal strata of different colors, from deep red to bright yellow.

"At night for the first time since leaving Pawnee Fork, I was interrupted for a moment in my observations, by moisture on the glass of my horizontal shade, showing a degree of humidity in the atmosphere not before existing. . . The effect of the night's dampness was felt in the morning, for, although the thermometer was only thirty-seven degrees, the cold was more sensible than in the dry regions at twenty-five degrees."*

* "Notes of a Military Reconnoissance."

In leaving the mountains, where the grass was a set-off for rugged obstacles, the want of it became a serious danger. On the 9th, they fell upon fresh trails of horses, which they supposed might be those of General Castro, who, Carson had informed them, was to go to Sonora,—of which the settlements were not distant—for recruits, and to return.

Casa de Montezuma.

November 10th.—"The valley on the southern side of the Gila still grows wider. About the time of the noon halt, a large pile, which seemed the work of human hands, was seen to the left. It was the remains of a three story mud house, sixty feet square, pierced for doors and windows. The walls four feet thick, and formed by layers of mud two feet thick; it was no doubt built by the same race that had once thickly peopled this territory, and left behind the ruins.

"The charred ends of the cedar joists were still in the wall. I examined them, and found they had not been cut with a steel instrument; the joists were round sticks; there were four entrances—the doors about four feet by two—the rooms had the same arrangement on each story; there was no sign of a fireplace in the building; the walls had been smoothed outside and plastered inside, and the surface still remained firm, although it was evident they had been exposed to great heat from the fire. There were the remains of the walls of four buildings, and the piles of earth showing where many others had been. A few yards further was a terrace one hundred yards by seventy, upon this was a pyramid about eight feet high, and twenty-five yards square at top. From this, sitting on my horse, I could overlook the vast plain, on the left bank of the Gila; the ground in view was about fifteen miles, all of which, it would seem, had been irrigated by the waters of the Gila. I picked up a broken crystal of quartz in one of these piles. Leaving the 'casa,' I turned towards the Pimos, and travelling at random over the plain, now covered with mezquit, the piles of earth and pottery showed for hours in every direction. I also found the remains of a zequia, which followed the range of houses for miles. It had been very large. When I got to camp, I found them on good grass and in communication with the Pimos, who came out with a frank welcome. Their answer to Carson, when he went up and asked for provisions, was 'bread is to eat, not to sell, take what you want.' The General asked a Pimo who made the house I had seen. 'It is the Casa de Montezuma;' said he, 'It was built by the son of the most beautiful woman, who once dwelt in yon mountain; she was fair, and all the handsome men came to court her, but in vain; when they came they paid tribute, and out of this small store she fed all the people in times of famine, and it did not diminish. At last as she lay asleep, a drop of rain fell upon her navel, and she became pregnant, and brought forth a boy who was the builder of all these houses.' He seemed unwilling to talk about them, but said there were many more of them to the north, south-west, etc.; ... he said this casa had been burnt too long ago for any of them to remember." *

I venture an opinion which ardent archæologists may scout, that we need only look to the not very remote ancestry of the tribes now found in Zuñi, Acoma, etc., and the Pueblos of New Mexico,—as Pecos and San Domingo,—for the architects and inhabiters of all these ruins and remains.

* Journal of Captain A. R. Johnston, First Dragoons, A. D. C.

The General obtained of the Pimos a sufficiency of corn and wheat and beans, but only two or three bullocks, and no mules or horses. They had only steers for tillage, procured from the Mexicans.

"To us it was a rare sight to be thrown in the midst of a large nation of what are termed wild Indians, surpassing many of the Christian nations in agriculture, little behind them in the useful arts, and immeasurably before them in honesty and virtue. During the whole of yesterday, our camp was full of men, women, and children, who sauntered among our packs, unwatched, and not a single instance of theft was reported."*

The Maricopas, some on foot, but mostly on horseback, came at full speed to their lower camp; unarmed and in the most confident manner, bringing watermelons, meal, pinole and salt,—this last taken from the plains. A pair of spectacles was a cause of much amusement; the women had an idea that the wearer could see through their cotton blankets, but at length a pair being put upon an old woman, she became acquainted with their use, and explained it to the others.

* "Notes of a Military Reconnoissance."

November 14th and 15th, the General made the jornada of forty-three miles across the bend of the Gila, losing six or eight mules from exhaustion, and want of water. They halted then a day, and found the remains of a zequia and much broken pottery. It was probably the work of the Maricopas, who are known to have moved gradually up from the Gulf.

November 22d.—" Most of the men were on foot, and a small party composed chiefly of the General and staff, were a long way ahead of the straggling column, when, as we approached the end of our day's journey, every man was straightened in his saddle by our suddenly falling on a camp, which from the trail, we estimated at one thousand men, who must have left that morning. Speculation was rife, but we all soon settled down upon the opinion that it was General Castro and his troops; that he had succeeded in recruiting an army in Sonora, and was now on his return to California. Carson expressed his belief that he must be only ten miles below, at the crossing. Our force consisted of only one hundred and ten men. The General decided we were too few to be attacked, and must be the aggressive party, and if Castro's camp could be found, that he would attack it the moment night set in, and beat them before it was light enough to discover our force.

"The position of our camp was decided, as usual, with reference to the grass. The lives of our animals were nearly as important as our own."*

A party was sent at dark, and it succeeded in capturing four Mexicans. It turned out that the alarm had been caused by a few soldiers and others, and their drove of five hundred horses from California, for the use of Castro in Sonora. The four men, examined separately, told each a different story. One of them, tall and venerable in appearance, reported himself to be the poor employé of a rich man supplying the Sonora market with horses. It was afterwards ascertained that he was a colonel of the Mexican army.

The General remained there next day, attempting to remount his escort from the captured horses. And then a courier with a mail from California fell into his hands; he bore letters to General Castro and other men of note in Sonora, and thus Kearny was informed of the counter revolution in California.

* "Notes of a Military Reconnoissance."

"Captain Flores was named as the general and governor *pro tem.*, and the enthusiasm of the people was described as overflowing in the cause of emancipation from the Yankee yoke. One letter gave a minute and detailed account of a victory stated to have been obtained over the Americans. It stated that four hundred and fifty men landed at San Pedro, and were met, defeated, and driven back to the fort at San Pedro. . . We also learned that the horses captured were in part for General Castro. Nothing more was wanting to legitimize our capture, and Captain Moore was directed to remount his men."*

The Mexicans were very dexterous in evading inquiries; one of them, an acquaintance of Carson, was well plied with brandy; but the most that could be extorted from him, was the advice not to march directly upon Los Angeles.

"The captured horses were all wild and but little adapted for immediate service; but there was rare sport in catching them, and we saw for the first time the lazo thrown with inimitable skill. It is a saying in Chihuahua that a 'Californian can throw

* "Notes of a Military Reconnoissance."

the lazo as well with his foot as the Mexican can with his hand,' and the scene before us gave us an idea of its truth. There was a wild stallion of great beauty which defied the fleetest horse and the most expert rider. At length a boy of fourteen, a Californian, whose graceful riding was a constant subject of admiration, piqued by repeated failures, mounted a fresh horse, and followed by an Indian, launched fiercely at the stallion.

His lariat darted from his hand with the force and precision of a rifle ball, and rested on the neck of the fugitive; the Indian, at the same moment, made a successful throw, but the stallion was too stout for both, and dashed off at full speed, with both ropes flying in the air like wings. The perfect representation of Pegasus, he took a sweep, and followed by his pursuers, came thundering down the dry bed of the river. The lazos were now trailing on the ground, and the gallant young Spaniard, taking advantage of the circumstance, stooped from his flying horse and caught one in his hand. It was the work of a moment to make it fast to the pommel of his saddle, and by a short turn of his own horse, he threw the stallion a complete somersault, and the game was secure."*

November 25th, the river was forded at the same place, ten miles below the Gila's mouth, that the Mormon battalion passed forty-six days later, some of the horses swimming when its crooked course was lost; they camped fifteen miles below, at the first well, where only the men got water. Next day they reached the Alamo Mocho well, twenty-four miles, at 4 P. M.; they had much work to deepen the well before water was reached; an old champagne basket, first, and then a basket work of willow twigs, was used to prevent caving sand. The evening and night were spent in watering the animals, which had made two marches without drinking.

The following morning they marched very early, and in forty miles reached at 8 o'clock P. M. a salt lake, of which contradictory accounts had been received; it was found surrounded by a thick quagmire, and the water wholly unfit for any use. After a few hours' rest, the animals browsing at a few mezquit trees, they marched on in the dark, but

* "Notes of a Military Reconnoissance."

were favored after sunrise, by a heavy fog for two hours, which proved refreshing; but "the stoutest animals now began to stagger, and when day dawned scarcely a man was seen mounted." At noon the Cariza was reached.

November 29, the grass being bad, and rations nearly exhausted, the march was continued at a "snail's pace," and that night a horse was killed for food, which was eaten with great appetite, and all of it consumed. They were compelled to remain in camp next day.

December 2d, the General arrived at Warner's rancho, and learned "that the Mexicans were still in the possession of the whole country except San Diego, San Francisco, and Monterey; that we were near the heart of the enemy's stronghold, whence he drew his supplies of men, cattle, and horses, and that we were now in possession of the great pass to Sonora, by which he expected to retreat if defeated, to send his prisoners if successful, and to communicate with Mexico.

"To appease hunger, however, was the first consideration. Seven of my men ate at one single meal, a fat full grown sheep."

A Mr. Stokes, who lived fifteen miles on the road to San Diego, was sent for and came; "his dress was a black velvet English hunting coat, a pair of black velvet trowsers, cut off at the knees and open on the outside to the hip, beneath which were drawers of spotless white; his leggings were of black buckskin, and his heels armed with spurs six inches long. Above the whole bloomed the merry face of Mr Stokes, the Englishman. He was very frank, proclaimed himself a neutral, but gave all the information he possessed, which was, that Commodore Stockton was in possession of San Diego, and that all the country between that place and Santa Barbara was in possession of the 'country people;' he stated he was going to San Diego the next morning. The General gave him a letter for that place."*

Information was received that there was a band of horses and mules fifteen miles on the road to Los Angeles, belonging to General Flores. Lieutenant Davidson and fifteen men, accompanied by Carson, were sent at nightfall to capture them. The party returned successful next day, December 3d, at noon;

* " Notes of a Military Reconnoissance."

but the animals were found to be mostly unbroken, and so, little serviceable.

December 4th.—The General marched in a rain which lasted all day; he camped at Mr. Stokes' place, in the valley of the San Isabel River, which was formerly a mission.

Next day they marched to the rancheria of Santa Maria ; where it was learned that the enemy was in force, nine miles distant ; it was after dark, but there being no grass, they went two miles further and camped in a cañon. On the way they met Captain Gillespie, Lieutenant Beale, and Midshipman Duncan of the navy, with a party of thirty-five men, sent from San Diego with a dispatch for General Kearny.

The following is from the General's official report :—

"Having learned from Captain Gillespie, of the volunteers, that there was an armed party of Californians at San Pascual, three leagues distant, . . . I sent Lieutenant Hammond, First Dragoons, with a few men to make a reconnoissance of them. He returned at two in the morning of the 6th instant, reporting that he had found the party in the place mentioned, and that he had been seen, though not pursued by them. I then determined that I would march for, and attack them by break of day; arrangements were accordingly made for the purpose. My aid-de-camp, Captain Johnston, First Dragoons, was assigned to the command of the advanced guard of twelve dragoons mounted on the best horses we had; then followed about fifty dragoons under Captain Moore, mounted, but, with few exceptions, on the tired mules they had ridden from Santa Fè, ten hundred and fifty miles; then about twenty volunteers of Captain Gibson's company under his command and that of Captain Gillespie; then followed our two mountain howitzers with dragoons to manage them, and under the command of Lieutenant Davidson of the regiment. . . As the day, December 6th, dawned, we approached the enemy at San Pascual, who was already in the saddle, when Captain Johnston made a furious charge upon them with his advanced guard, and was in a short time after supported by the dragoons, soon after which the enemy gave way, having kept up from the beginning a continual fire upon us. Upon the retreat of the enemy, Captain Moore led off rapidly in pursuit, accompanied by the dragoons mounted on horses, and was followed, though slowly, by the others on their tired mules. The enemy, well mounted and among the best horsemen in the world, after retreating about half a mile, and seeing an interval between Captain Moore with his advance and the dragoons coming to his support, rallied their whole force, charged with their lances, and on account of their greatly-superior numbers, but few of us in front remained untouched;* for five minutes they held the ground from us, when our men coming up, we again drove them, and they fled from the field not to return to it, which we occupied and encamped upon. A most melancholy duty now remains for me; it is to report the death of my aid-de-camp, Captain Johnston, who was shot dead at the commencement of the action; of Captain Moore, who was lanced just previous to the final retreat of the enemy; and of Lieutenant Hammond, also lanced, who survived but a few hours. We also had killed, two sergeants, two corporals, and ten privates of the first dragoons; one private of the volunteers, and one engaged in the topographical department.

* Their number was thirty-eight; *all* of whom save two, were killed or wounded.

Among the wounded are myself, (in two places) Lieutenant Warner, topographical engineers, (in three places,) Captain Gillespie and Captain Gibson, of the volunteers, (the former in three places,) one sergeant, bugler and nine privates of the dragoons; many of them receiving from two to ten lance wounds, most of them when unhorsed and incapable of resistance. Our howitzers were not brought into the action, but coming to the front at the close of it, before they were turned so as to admit of being fired upon the retreating enemy, the two mules before one of them got alarmed and freeing themselves from their drivers ran off among the enemy and were thus lost to us. The enemy proved to be a party of about one hundred and sixty Californians, under Andreas Pico, brother of the late governor."

Thanks are returned for their gallantry, particularly to Captain Turner, first dragoons, A. A. A. G., and to Lieutenant Emory. The General's wounds were so serious, that during the day Captain Turner was in command; the ground was so rough with rocks and cacti, that it was difficult to find a smooth place even for the wounded. The dead were buried that night, as secretly as possible, for fear of the disturbance and robbery of the bodies, "with no other accompaniment than the howlings of myriads of wolves."

Early in the day messengers had been sent, by a circuitous route, to San Diego, thirty-nine miles distant, for wheel carriages for the use of the wounded.

" Our provisions were exhausted, our horses dead,

our mules on their last legs, and our men, now reduced to one-third of their number, were ragged, worn down by fatigue, and emaciated." *

The General's report continues:—

"On the morning of the 7th, having made ambulancse for our wounded . . . we proceeded on our march, when the enemy showed himself, occupying the hills in our front, which they left as we approached, till reaching San Bernardo a party of them took possession of a hill near to it and maintained their position until attacked by our advance, who quickly drove them from it, killing and wounding five of their number with no loss on our part."

The captured hill was kept possession of; the cattle had been lost in this attack.

December 8th, water was bored for, and the fattest of the mules was killed for meat. That day, under a flag of truce, one of the messengers to San Diego captured on his return, was exchanged. It was understood that these messengers brought back a written refusal of aid; certainly no aid came; the exchanged man stated he had hid a dispatch at a certain tree pointed out; but the dispatch could not, afterward, be found. It was twenty-nine miles to San Diego. It was impossible to remove the wounded until they could ride, in the presence of such superior numbers, and that night Lieutenant Beale, of the

* "Notes of a Military Reconnoissance."

Navy,* Carson, and an Indian, volunteered and went to San Diego; it was a dangerous undertaking, as the enemy occupied all the roads. That day "the brave Sergeant Cox," who had died of his wounds, was buried.

Two more days passed without aid for this crippled, encumbered band,—surrounded by an increasing horde of enemies. December 10th, "The enemy attacked our camp, driving before them a band of wild horses, with which they hoped to produce a stampede. Our men behaved with admirable coolness, turning off the wild animals dexterously. Two or three of the fattest were killed in the charge, and formed, in the shape of a gravy-soup, an agreeable substitute for the poor steaks of our worn down brutes, on which we had been feeding for a number of days.†

* Since Minister to Austria.

† "Notes of a Military Reconnoissance." The following is also extracted,—occurring the night of the 8th: "Don Antonio Robideaux, a thin man of fifty-five years, slept next to me. The loss of blood from his wounds, added to the coldness of the night, twenty-eight degrees Fahrenheit, made me think he would never see daylight, but I was mistaken. He woke me to ask if I did not smell coffee, and expressed the belief that a cup of that beverage would save his life, and that nothing else would. Not knowing that there had been any coffee in camp for many days, I supposed a dream had carried him back to the cafés of St Louis and New Orleans, and it was with some surprise that I found my cook heating a cup of coffee

NEW MEXICO AND CALIFORNIA. 261

The same day the surgeon, Griffin, reported that all the wounded but two, would be able to ride.

There was so little expectation of Lieutenant Beale's success that the General ordered every incumbrance including great-coats, to be burned; and all preparation to be made for the march next morning.

"We were all reposing quietly, but not sleeping, waiting for the break of day, when we were to go down and give the enemy another defeat. . . . The tramp of a column was heard, followed by the hail of a sentinel.

"It was a detachment of one hundred tars and eighty marines under Lieutenant Gray, sent to meet us by Commodore Stockton, from whom we learned that Lieutenant Beale, Carson and the Indian

---

over a small fire made of wild sage. One of the most agreeable little offices performed in my life, and I believe in the cook's, to whom the coffee belonged, was to pour the precious draught into the waning body of our friend Robideaux. His warmth returned, and with it hopes of life. In gratitude he gave me the half of a cake made of brown flour, almost black with dirt, and which had, for greater security, been hidden in the clothes of his Mexican servant, a man who scorned ablutions. I ate more than half without inspection, when, on breaking a piece, the bodies of several of the most loathsome insects were exposed to my view. My hunger, however, overcame my fastidiousness, and the morceau did not appear particularly disgusting."

had arrived safely in San Diego. The detachment left San Diego on the night of the 9th, cached themselves during the day of the 10th, and joined us on the night of that day. These gallant fellows busied themselves till day distributing their provisions and clothes to our naked and hungry people." *

This junction was a surprise to the Californians, and when the sun rose on the 11th, only a squad of them was to be seen; and in retiring they had left most of the cattle behind, although none of General Kearny's force were now mounted. It was ascertained that one hundred and eighty Californians were engaged at San Pascual, and that one hundred additional joined them next day from the Pueblo of Los Angeles.

December 12th, General Kearny reached San Diego.

The frigate Congress and sloop Portsmouth were at the anchorage opposite the hide ware-houses two miles from the village; this consisted of a few adobe houses, only two or three, of all, with plank floors.

* "Notes of a Military Reconnoissance."

V.

FINAL CONQUEST OF CALIFORNIA.

THUS General Kearny had found that the Californians, having thought better of their first apparent submission—which was the result of surprise, and their habitual acquiescence in pronunciamentos and revolutions—had thrown off, by force of arms, near three months previously, the foreign yoke; that of the whole great Territory, only three small villages on the coast were dominated by the navy, which had ceased all further efforts, apparently vain enough. He had fought the first battle of the real conquest.

Now his first thoughts were not of title, of rank, and right of command in the Territory, but patriotic and unselfish. His lance wounds soon healing, he suggested and then patiently continued to urge on Commodore Stockton that action must be taken; that the naval force which could be spared to act on land, his few dragoons and some volunteers should attempt a campaign; should march into the heart of the most inimical district, and attack and recover the capital, the Ciudad de Los Angeles.

He finally prevailed, and Commodore Stockton consented.

December 29th, 1846, General Kearny and Commodore Stockton marched from San Diego with near six hundred men; they were composed of about sixty dismounted dragoons, sixty volunteers, including some Indians, and the rest sailors and marines. There was a battery of six pieces of various calibre, drawn by oxen, and a baggage train of eleven ox-carts: the acting infantry force was divided into four bodies, commanded by Captain Turner, Lieutenant Renshaw, Navy, Lieutenants Zielin and Gillespie, Marine Corps; the artillery by Lieutenant Tilghman, of the Navy.

The march and camps were habitually in a hollow square, with cattle and baggage in the centre, artillery at the angles. They camped at the first watering place, the Solidad, at 8 o'clock, P. M. Captain Emory as adjutant-general, had been "ordered to ride forward and lay out a defensive camp, hoping to give confidence to the sailors, many of whom were now for the first time, transferred to a new element."*

The march was ten or twelve miles a day.

January 4th, nine miles beyond Flores, they approached a defile of eight miles, the road being thrown on the sea beach by high lands; they were there met by a flag of truce, bearing a letter from Flores, styling himself governor and captain-general of the department of California, proposing to suspend hostilities in the department, and leave the battle to be fought elsewhere upon which was to depend the fate of California between the United States and Mexico. The commission was dismissed with a peremptory refusal of the proposition. Fortunately the little army found low tide and marched upon the hard beaten sand; they met no opposition, and passed beyond, making eighteen miles that day.

January 6th, after a long march camp was made at the upper Santa Anna, which was deserted by all except a few old women, who had *bolted their doors*; "such was the unanimity of the men, women

* " Notes of a Military Reconnoissance."

and children, in support of the war, that not a particle of information could be obtained in reference to the enemy's force or position."

At 2 o'clock, January 8th, the army came in sight of the San Gabriel River, where the enemy began to show themselves. "The river was about one hundred yards wide, knee deep, and flowing over quicksand ; either side was fringed with a thick undergrowth. The approach on our side was level, that on the enemy's side favorable to him. A bank fifty feet high ranged parallel with the river, at point blank distances, upon which he posted his artillery."*

General Kearny's account of the action which followed is embraced in his short official report to the Adjutant-General, which should be here given entire.

Headquarters Army of the West, Ciudad de Los Angeles,
Upper California, January 12, 1847.

SIR,—I have the honor to report, that at the request of Commodore R. F. Stockton (who in September last assumed the title of Governor of California), I consented to take command of an expedition to this place—capital of the country—and that on the 29th of December, I left San Diego with about

---

* "Notes of a Military Reconnoissance."

five hundred men, consisting of sixty dismounted dragoons, under Captain Turner; fifty California volunteers, and the remainder of marines and sailors, with a battery of artillery. Lieutenant Emory, topographical engineers, acted as assistant adjutant-general. Commodore Stockton accompanied us. We proceeded on our route without seeing the enemy till the 8th instant, when they showed themselves in full force of six hundred mounted men, with four pieces of artillery, under their Governor Flores, occupying the heights in front of us, which commanded the crossing of the river San Gabriel, and they ready to oppose our further progress. The necessary disposition of our troops was immediately made, by covering our front with a strong party of skirmishers, placing our wagons and baggage train in rear of them, and protecting the flanks and rear with the remainder of the command. We then proceeded, forded the river, carried the heights, and drove the enemy from them after an action of about one and a half hours, during which they made a charge upon our left flank, which was repulsed; soon after which, they retreated and left us in possession of the field, on which we encamped that night.

The next day, the 9th instant, we proceeded on our march at the usual hour, the enemy in front and on our flanks, and when we reached the plains of the Mesa, their artillery again opened upon us, when their fire was returned by our guns as we advanced; and after hovering around and near us for about two hours, occasionally skirmishing with us during that time, they concentrated their force and made another charge on our left flank, which was quickly repulsed; shortly after which they retired, we continuing our march; and in the afternoon encamped on the bank of the San Fernando, three miles below this city, which we entered the following morning without molestation.

Our loss in the actions of the 8th and 9th instant was small, being one private killed and two officers (Lieutenant Renshaw of the navy and Captain Gillespie of the volunteers) and eleven privates wounded. The enemy mounted on fine horses and being the best riders in the world, carried off their killed and wounded, and we know not the number of them, though it must have been considerable.

    Very respectfully your obedient servant,
      S. W. KEARNY, Brigadier-General.
To Brigadier-General R. Jones,
  Adjutant-General United States Army, Washington.

In fact, while marching on the city, on the 10th, a flag of truce was met, and a verbal agreement was made of surrender on condition of respecting persons and property.

The town was deserted by many of its regular inhabitants; but the streets were found " full of desperate and drunken fellows, who brandished their arms and saluted us with .every term of reproach. The crest, overlooking the town, in rifle range, was covered with horsemen, engaged in the same hospitable manner . . . the Californians on the hill, did fire on the vaqueros. The rifles were then ordered to clear the hill, which a single fire effected, killing two of the enemy. . . Towards the close of the day we learned very certainly that Flores, with one hundred and fifty men, chiefly Sonorians, and desperadoes of the country, had fled toward Sonora, taking with him four or five hundred of the best horses and mules of the country, the property of his own friends."*

  * " Notes of a Military Reconnoissance."

Next day Lieutenant Emory was ordered to select a site, and commence a fort capable of defence by one hundred men, and commanding the town; it was begun, but the work was continued only for a few days. Many men came into Los Angeles and surrendered themselves.

Lieutenant-Colonel Fremont was left at the mission of San Fernando, January 11th, about twenty-four miles from Los Angeles, having been six weeks on his march from San Juan, near Monterey.

That same day two Californians met the battalion, and gave information of the two days' fighting, and that General Kearny and Commodore Stockton had marched into Los Angeles the day before. "A little farther on, we met a Frenchman who stated that he was the bearer of a letter from General Kearny, at Los Angeles, to Colonel Fremont. He confirmed the statement we had just heard."*

On the morning of the 13th, two Californian officers arrived at the mission, to treat of peace, and a consultation was held. The same day the battalion marched to the rancho of Couenga, twelve miles,

* "What I saw in California," by E. Bryant, p. 391.

—half way to Los Angeles. There, terms of capitulation and peace were agreed upon, viz.

ARTICLES OF CAPITULATION made and entered into at the rancho of Couenga, this thirteenth day of January, eighteen hundred and forty-seven, between P. B. Reading, Major Louis McLane, Jr., commanding Third Artillery; William H. Russell, ordnance officer—commissioners appointed, by J. C. Fremont, Colonel United States Army, and Military commandant of California; and Jose Antonio Carrillo, Commandant squadron; Augustin Olivera, deputado—Commissioners appointed by Don Andreas Pico, Commander-in-chief of the Californian forces under the Mexican flag.

Article 1st.—The commissioners on the part of the Californians, agree that their entire force shall, on presentation of themselves to Lieutenant-colonel Fremont, deliver up their artillery and public arms, and that they shall return peaceably to their homes, conforming to the laws and regulations of the United States, and not again take up arms during the war between the United States and Mexico, but will assist and aid in placing the country in a state of peace and tranquillity.

Article 2d.—The commissioners on the part of Lieutenant-colonel Fremont agree and bind themselves, on the fulfilment of the first article by the Californians, that they shall be guaranteed protection of life and property, whether on parole or otherwise.

Article 3d.—That until a treaty of peace be made and signed between the United States of North America, and the Republic of Mexico, no Californian, or any other Mexican citizen shall be bound to take the oath of allegiance.

Article 4th.—That any Californian or citizen of Mexico, desiring, is permitted by this capitulation, to leave the country without let or hindrance.

Article 5th.—That in virtue of the aforesaid articles, equal rights and privileges are vouchsafed to every citizen of California as are enjoyed by the citizens of the United States of North America.

Article 6th.—All officers, citizens, foreigners, and others, shall receive the protection guaranteed by the Second Article.

Article 7th.—This capitulation is intended to be no bar in effecting such arrangement as may in future be in justice required by both parties.

Ciudad de Los Angeles, Jan. 16th, 1847.

ADDITIONAL ARTICLE.—That the paroles of all officers, citizens, and others of the United States and of naturalized citizens of Mexico, are by this foregoing capitulation cancelled, and every condition of said paroles, from and after this date, are of no further force and effect, and all prisoners of both parties are hereby released.

    P. B. READING, Major, Cal'a Battalion.
    LOUIS MCLANE, Commander Artillery.
    WM. H. RUSSELL, Ordnance Officer.
    JOSE ANTONIO CARRILLO, Comd't of Squadron.
    AUGUSTIO OLIVERA, Deputado.

Approved,

    J. C. FREMONT, Lieut.-colonel, U. S. Army, and Military Commandant of California.
    ANDRES PICO, Commandant of Squadron, and Chief of the National Forces of California.

On the 14th, Lieutenant-Colonel Fremont marched his volunteer battalion into Los Angeles, and there placed them in temporary quarters. The capitulation would appear not to have been signed or approved until after his junction with the forces of General Kearny and Commodore Stockton.

The following is taken from an official report of Commodore Stockton to the Secretary of the Navy, dated January 15th, 1847:

"José Ma. Flores, the commander of the insurgent forces, two or three days previous to the 8th, sent two commissioners with a flag of truce to my camp to make a 'treaty of peace.' I informed the commissioners that I could not recognize Jose Ma. Flores, who had broken his parole, as an honorable man, or as one having any rightful authority, worthy to be treated with, that he was a rebel in arms, and if I caught him I would have him shot. It seems that not being able to negotiate with me, and having lost the battles of the 8th and 9th, they met Colonel Fremont on the 12th instant, on his way here, who not knowing what had occurred, he entered into capitulation with them, which I now send to you; and, although I refused to do it myself, still I have thought it best to approve it."

The fact that Lieutenant-colonel Fremont did not treat with the objectionable Flores, must make it certain that Commodore Stockton referred, in this report, to the only matter of importance, that Lieutenant-colonel Fremont made a treaty, with enemies he had never met, in a camp twelve miles from the capital and the headquarters of two superiors in rank and civil authority, who had recently fought and defeated them. And the facts shown, make it evident that Lieutenant-colonel Fremont did "know what had occurred," and that Commodore R. F. Stockton knew that it was so.

The Secretary of War, in his instructions to General Kearny, dated June 3d, 1846, informs him, "It is expected that the naval forces of the United

States which are now, or will soon be in the Pacific, will be in possession of all the towns of the sea coast, and will co-operate with you in the conquest of California," and further; "should you conquer and take possession of New Mexico and Upper California, or considerable places in either, you will establish temporary civil governments therein."

The Secretary of the Navy, in communicating instructions addressed to Commodore Stockton, dated November 5th, 1846, says:

" The President has deemed it best for the public interests to invest the military officer commanding with the direction of the operations on land, and with the administrative functions of government over the people and territory occupied by us. You will relinquish to Colonel Mason, or to General Kearny, if the latter shall arrive before you have done so, the entire control over these matters, and turn over to him all papers necessary to the performance of his duties."

He had previously, July 12th, 1846, instructed the commander of the naval forces: "For your further instruction I enclose you a copy of confidential instructions from the War Department to Brigadier S. W. Kearny, who is ordered, overland, to California. You will also communicate your instructions to him, and inform him that they have the sanction of the President."

And August 13th, the Secretary of the Navy instructed "The senior officer in command of the United States naval forces in the Pacific Ocean;— The President expects and requires, however, the most cordial and effectual coöperation between the officers of the two services, in taking possession of, and holding the ports and positions of the enemy, which are designated in the instructions to either or both branches of the service, and will hold any commander of either branch to a strict responsibility for any failure to preserve harmony and secure the objects proposed."

General Kearny having now, by the accession of Fremont's battalion, sufficient forces for service on land, asserted his rights, as necessary for the performance of the duties which had been intrusted to him, to "establish civil governments." Lieutenant colonel Fremont refused to report to him, or to obey his orders; and in this he was evidently supported by Commodore Stockton.

General Kearny was, for the time, utterly powerless, and on the 18th of January set out with his dragoon escort for San Diego, and sent Captain Emory, by Panama, with dispatches for Washington.

Next day, Commodore Stockton appointed Lieutenant-colonel Fremont, Governor of California, and set out, also, for San Diego where his squadron lay; and the day following the sailors and marines marched to embark at San Pedro to rejoin their ships.

January 22d Lieutenant-colonel Fremont, as "Governor and Commander-in-chief of California," proclaimed "order and peace restored to the country."

Commodore Stockton, in his latter years, was accounted by many as erratic, and at times beyond the verge of reason.

But how shall be explained this dangerous indulgence of a spurious ambition, by a character, whom the people of the United States saw fit afterward to place in very great prominence? Did he have unbounded trust in an influence which had shown such friendly potency in the outset of his California career?

Do the Spainards take every where a moral contagion? or does the arid atmosphere of their chosen abodes,—in Mexico, in California, as in Spain, —so peculiarly affect the brains of men, as to make these countries the lands of pronunciamentos and anarchy? *

* All the world knows that an investigation that same year of

Hostilities were not confined to Southern California. While General Kearny was marching on Los Angeles, one Don Francisco Sanchez, at the head of a hundred men, held sway for a time in the country about San Francisco and Monterey. Besides other Americans whom he held prisoners, he captured Lieut. Bartlett, of the Navy, acting alcalde of San Francisco. Then Captain Marston, Marine corps, was sent against him from San Francisco, with one hundred marines and volunteers, and a piece of artillery. January 2d, he met him on the plains of Santa Clara; after an action of an hour, with small loss on either side, Sanchez retreated and the same evening sent by a flag, a request for an armistice and conference. Next day Marston was joined by a company of mounted volunteers, under Lieut. Maddox, Marine corps, from Monterey.

January 8th, the Californians gave up Lieutenant Bartlett and other prisoners, surrendered a field-piece and other arms, and disbanded.

Col. F.'s conduct at this time by a general court martial, resulted in his conviction of mutiny and disobedience of orders, and sentence of dismissal from the army.

Commodore Stockton escaped a trial.

Dangerous Consequences of the Mutiny.
An Interregnum.

THE narrative of the march of the infantry battalion under Lieutenant-colonel Cooke, was closed at its arrival at the Mission of San Diego, January 29th, 1847, and his report in person to General Kearny the same evening at San Diego.

General Kearny could in no way authorize recognition of the usurpation then existing; he instructed Lieut.-colonel Cooke to march to the mission of San Luis Rey, fifty-three miles from San Diego, on the road to Los Angeles, and there to quarter his battalion; to await events and further orders, but to exercise such authority and power as might become necessary in his judgment, under unforeseen circumstances of national interests and defence.

Most fortunately, Commodore Shubrick was then expected at Monterey, as commander of the Pacific squadron. The opportunity of a vessel of war sailing the next day for Monterey, offering itself, General Kearny embarked, January 30th, for that port.

Lieut.-colonel Cooke was thus left in the command of the only troops in California that had been mustered into the service of the United States; a few dragoons, and a battalion of volunteers, which up to that time had never had opportunity to receive regular instruction in arms.

Lieutenant-colonel Fremont,—eighty-eight miles north of San Luis Rey,—was in command of a "battalion," only provisionally in the service; of men more ignorant of military law and discipline than their commander, (who had never served but as a detached topographical engineer,) but they were personally dependent on him and devoted to his fortunes; and Fremont claimed absolute authority, civil and military, in the Territory.

But to complete the situation. A few days before a body of enemies superior in number to both battalions,—half savage and raised to arms,—quite accustomed to seditions and revolutions, had disbanded under a capitulation made under the depression of their defeat, but without much loss, by large forces which then, near by, held their capital. That force had now been reduced to the small undisciplined battalion of Fremont. These insurgents knew well the dissensions and divided authority among their enemies; they had retained their arms, and were now, professedly, only waiting expected reinforcements from Mexico to renew the war.

The battalion accordingly marched to San Luis Rey, and took quarters in the Mission buildings, in the first days of February. The mission is beautifully situated, overlooking fertile and well watered lands; even the high hills showing, by their smoothness, the former cultivation, in wheat. It is only two or three miles distant, but does not command a view of the ocean. This immense mission structure, with an imposing church in an angle, built about sixty years previously, was found in good condition; buildings, and corral and garden wall-tops as well, protected by roofs of red tiles. In the centre of the main court was an orange tree with ripening fruit; pomegranate trees were in their beautiful blossom. There were other courts,—one for cattle. The battalion found ample quarters. There was a large garden and vineyard, enclosed by handsome walls.

The absence of forest trees is a very characteristic feature of California; grey squirrels, which seemed identical with the tree species, were here found, but necessarily burrowing in the earth.

Lieut.-colonel Cooke immediately commenced a thorough practical instruction of the battalion in tactics; the absence of books made it a difficult and laborious task,—teaching and drilling officers half the day, and superintending, in the other half, their efforts to impart what they had just imperfectly learned. But all were in earnest, and in a very few weeks the complete battalion exercises were mastered.

The "Secretary of State" stopped at the mission the evening of February 21st; sent, he said from the capital to represent the government at a ball to be given February 22d, by Commodore Stockton at San Diego. He stated that two companies of Californians had been raised for service; that any attack to displace the present government would be resisted by force, that a thousand natives would rise to support Colonel Fremont. But his opinions and assertions were equally unreliable. But about that time there was good evidence that many inhabitants pretty openly asserted that they would rise again, if any assistance came from Sonoma.

Major Swords, Quarter-master, who was sent to

the Sandwich Islands for provisions and specie, arrived at San Diego February 19th with flour, sugar, etc.

In my diary I find for March 1st: "Last night two more families, passing, applied for the use of quarters, and several officers gave up to them their rooms. They have spent here much of the day. They travel in carts drawn by oxen; the 'mode' too at Constantinople and in New Mexico. But these carts are superior to the New Mexican's, and contain mattresses,—which with blanket awnings, must make them rather comfortable. The travelers were of the best class, and the ladies were handsome.

This contrast of ox carts to male locomotion here, is extreme. On our march I was startled by a party of men riding at full gallop to meet us, and driving twenty or thirty horses; it was one or two proprietors traveling, with their servants; then I saw two of the men dash into the drove, swinging their lazos, with which they caught two loose horses; very quickly they transferred the equipments of those they had ridden,—which were then turned loose to rest themselves—at the gallop!"

Next day, Señor Bandini, of San Diego, called;

—a member of the "legislative council;" it appeared from his statements that the Frigate *Congress* was about to sail; that there was a small troop of native volunteers at the place, whose commander had written by him—to Colonel Fremont—that they must speedily disperse, from want of provisions.

An officer and thirty-two men were sent from San Luis Rey, the following morning, March 3d, to take post there, for protection of the town and of a provision depot.

There were reports then, from two sources, of the approach of a force from Sonora.

The killing of a beef presented a characteristic trait of Californians; the vaquero pursuing the herd at full speed with lazo flying, catches one by a fore leg, and throws it with a tremendous shock: he then cuts its throat. The lazo is also used for the rare occasion of catching and milking a cow, which has to be tightly bound after being caught.

March 9th.—"A frost last night; many of the men, volunteers and dragoons, have long been barefooted! they march on guard barefooted; none have overcoats; the volunteers never had them; those of the dragoons were burnt. There is no public money, for pay, or for purchase of provisions. I feed four hundred men at a cost to government of four and a half cents a day each; this being the value of four pounds of beef. The Californians pay their Indian servants with aguadiente; a sort of fiery whiskey which they distil.

March 12*th*.--" For forty days I have commanded the legal forces in California,—the war still existing; and not pretending to the highest authority of any sort, have had no communication with any higher, or any other, military, naval, or civil. . . I have put a garrison in San Diego; the civil officers, ap pointed by a naval officer, otherwise refusing to serve; while a naval officer ashore, is styled by some, " Governor of San Diego."

General Kearny is supreme—somewhere up the coast; Colonel Fremont supreme at Pueblo de los Angeles; Commodore Stockton is " Commander in-chief " at San Diego;—Commodore Shubrick, the same at Monterey, and I, at San Luis Rey;—and we are all supremely poor; the government having no money and no credit; and we hold the Territory because Mexico is poorest of all.

I rode to the seashore this afternoon, ana saw the spouting of whales."

March 14th.—Major H. S. Turner, as Adjutant General, arrived at San Luis Rey, the bearer of news and an important document: the announcement, in both languages, of the assumption of government, and all legal authority, naval and military, by Commodore Shubrick and General Kearny, at Monterey, now the capital.

Commodore Shubrick arrived there January 23d, and February 1st, issued a general order, as Commander-in-chief; it announced the arrival of Captain Tompkins' company of United States Artillery, and discharged, with commendation and thanks, Maddox's volunteers.

This was some weeks before General Kearny's arrival at Monterey.

But now a "circular" was published, dated March 1st, signed by Commodore Shubrick, "Commander-in-chief of the Naval Forces," and General Kearny, "Brigadier-general and Governor of California." It announced that, "to the Commander-in-chief of the Naval Forces the President has assigned the regulation of the import trade, the conditions on which vessels of all nations, our own as well as foreign, may be admitted into the ports of the territory, and the establishment of all port regulations.

"To the commanding military officer the president has assigned the direction of the operations on land, and has invested him with administrative functions of government over the people and territory occupied by the forces of the United States."

This a recital of facts well known from the first.

There was further, the proclamation of General Kearny as Governor.

It was long; it "absolved all the inhabitants of California from any further allegiance to the Republic of Mexico, and will consider them as citizens of the United States." . . . "The Americans and Californians are now but one people; let us cherish one wish, one hope, and let that be for the peace and quiet of our country. Let us, as a band of brothers, unite and emulate each other in our exertions to benefit and improve this our beautiful, and which soon must be, our happy and prosperous home."

It contained scarcely any allusion to existing dissensions, and this probably was the reason that it did not end them; those most unselfishly devoted to the safety of public interests, felt the imperative policy of concealing them; they observed their effect as temptations to complications involving bloodshed, and a thorough alienation of a simple minded population, and possibly the advantage of the *uti possidetis* at the treaty of peace, the period of which was beyond any conjecture in California. The reader must have observed the almost permanent severance of communication with the eastern side of the continent; let him consider that Commodore Stockton seems to have been six or eight weeks officially ignorant of Commodore Shubrick's presence very far short of the other extremity of the territory itself.

Major Turner, who came by way of Los Angeles, was bearer of a general order, placing Lieut.-colonel Cooke in command of the southern half of California; and he informed him that he had brought orders to Lieut.-colonel Fremont to disband his battalion, but that those men desiring it, should be mustered into public service. If he failed to obey, Captain Turner was instructed to notify General Kearny at Monterey, by express.

Lieutenant-colonel Cooke immediately sent a courier to Colonel Fremont, to ascertain what number of the men had been mustered into service. The answer was by a "governor," through his "secretary of state," that none had consented to enter the public service; but as rumors of insurrection were rife, it was not deemed safe to disband them. He asked for no assistance, under the dangerous circumstances; but on the contrary, added that the "battalion would be amply sufficient for the safety of the artillery and ordnance stores."

Meantime Captain Turner had returned to Los Angeles, and there being convinced that Lieutenant-colonel Fremont did not intend to obey the orders, set out himself, express, for Monterey; this being made known from the many horses driven according to the custom, Lieutenant-colonel Fremont set out, half a day later, and rode to Monterey in four days; but on arriving there he found that Captain Turner had also arrived, several hours before him. Nevertheless, it appeared that Lieutenant-colonel Fremont satisfied General Kearny that he would obey orders, and was suffered to return.

But Lieutenant-colonel Cooke had decided to

march to Los Angeles, and he reached there the 23d of March ; he was politely met, at the edge of town, by Captain Gillespie, who informed him that Lieutenant-colonel Fremont had left for Monterey the day before. The battalion was formed in line in the main street ; then the dragoons were quartered in a government building, and the battalion went into camp in the edge of the town.

The same day the alcalde waited on Lieutenant-colonel Cooke and informed him of frequent depredations by Indians, and that by last accounts, they were in possession of his rancho, about thirty-five miles distant. Next morning, a Lieutenant and thirty dragoons, mounted, were sent to investigate the matter,—and to act according to circumstances.

The following is extracted from Lieutenant-colonel Cooke's diary, March 24th :—

"After breakfast I rode out to the San Gabriel mission ; it is a beautiful plain, somewhat undulating, eight miles to that point ; it is part of the great "Mesa," but there is a low ridge of green hills ; the pin grass I found most luxuriant. As I approached the base of the mountain, I came in view of the woods of the San Gabriel River and its pretty valley, or meadow-land. Some two miles this side, stands the old mission, to which water is brought by a canal. There were the usual appearances of old fields and plantations,—and olive trees, dates, cactus hedges, etc.; a good large church, with pilasters; the buildings looked dingy and dilapidated, and above all, very dirty; the heads and offal of slaughtered beeves were lying in disagreeable vicinity.

"I fell in, on the road, with a gentlemen who said he was the adjutant, and seemed very ignorant of the true state of affairs, and asked what was the difficulty between General Kearny and Commodore Stockton. He had not seen, he said, either the circular of the Governor and Commodore Shubrick, or Tenth Military Department Order No. Two, relative to the mustering the battalion into service, etc. I showed them to him. All the volunteers I saw, seemed very polite, and even friendly. I went in to see Captain Owens, in command of the battalion. Lieutenant Davidson and Assistant-surgeon Sanderson were with me the whole time; Captain Owens expressed the same ignorance of the circular and the order; I showed them to him; the order he looked at a long time, but I am very much mistaken if he turned the leaf (it was on two sides of a leaf). I mentioned that they were not really in the United States service, unless for the purpose of being marched to a point to be discharged; I said I had an idea of putting some of my battalion out there; he said there was no room for them, that there was not room enough for all the battalion (the adjutant had told me that the battalion was now two hundred and six in number). I asked the captain, who seemed very shy, to show me the buildings, etc. He conducted me through his room into the court, where I saw the artillery and examined it; I remarked to him that there were the two howitzers belonging to the dragoons, and asked Mr. Davidson if one of them was not so much out of order that it could not be taken to town? and then said to Captain Owens that I had directed that some mules should be brought out to take those two pieces in, to-day. He observed that he had received special orders from Colonel Fremont not to turn over *any* of the artillery to any one, and that he could not let it go. I told him that the government authorities, the general of the army and governor, had committed the command here to *me*, and asked him if he did not acknowledge the authority of the United States Government? He said it was hard to know what was the legal authority,—he knew none but Colonel Fremont; he regarded him as the chief military authority in this country. I asked him what could convince him? what evidence he wanted? I took out and read to him the printed circular and the Department Order; told him that these were the highest authorities by land and sea; told him that Colonel Mason had lately came out express with the fresh orders of the government; that Fremont himself had so far obeyed as to drop his title of governor, and had gone to Monterey to report himself. He said he did not know what Colonel Fremont had gone for; that he would soon return,—that he ranked me, and he did not know but what Colonel Fremont had received other orders since the date of order No. Two, etc., etc. I very coolly and in perfect temper, exhausted every information, every argument, every appeal to his patriotism,—every motive in this distant land, for obedience and union amidst enemies; pointed out the disastrous consequences likely to ensue to public interests and to persons, by this treasonable course. In vain; he had received Fremont's orders to obey none other, and nothing more would he do. He had offered to show me the orders, and I finally told him I would look at them. . . . It was a letter of instructions to Captain Owens; after stating he was about to make a tour to the northern district, on matters connected with his military duties, it proceeded to five or six paragraphs of special orders; one was to the effect that he was to obey the orders of no officers, not coming expressly from him; another that he was to retain charge of all the ordnance, and to deliver it to no corps without express orders from him.

The President of the United States, in person, would fail to get the artillery, or be obeyed by Captain Owens with his battalion, until Lieutenant-colonel Fremont gave the permission! I asked for pen and ink to take a copy of the orders; he declined. I told Captain Owens that it was an illegal order; that we all bound ourselves to obey the legal orders of our superiors; and that Colonel Fremont could not defeat, or release the obligation. I told him I had no personal motives; that I only looked upon him as an American, whom I met as a friend far from home, and advised him, by my experience of twenty years' service, to think better of it. All was vain; these people, very many of them good well-meaning citizens have, it would seem, been cruelly and studiously deceived. . . . I took my leave."*

The "Secretary of State" disappeared at the approach of the battalion, leaving a report that he had left for the United States; a number of horses also had been taken from the mission; but there was evidence of his still being somewhere about Los Angeles.

March 25th.—The severe frosts óf the early part

---

* The late Hon. T. H. Benton, as advocate, and as Senator, in his many speeches against General Kearny, made the point that the author had in some way, been instructed by him to "crush" Lieutenant-colonel Fremont; the failure only arising from the author's imputed want of force of character. But as Colonel Fremont had disappeared at his approach—had gone to report to his legal commander—allusion must have been made to the author's brooking the mutinous conduct of the ignorant Owens.

Could insanity have gone farther than that a half of the diminutive forces holding the doubtful conquest of so distant a province, should resort to force of arms (evidently unnecessary, as the event, easily foreseen, proved) against the other half, and in the presence of armed and eager enemies!

The "conveniently missing" diary was also remarked upon. It had been sunk in crossing a river, near Sutter's Fort; but having been searched for, and found by Sutter's Indians, had not then been received or heard from.

of this month were unexampled, for any season of the year; it appeared that the young orange trees were much injured; and citrons, bearing at once flowers and fruit, were to be seen frost-bitten to near the root. But the orange groves of the vicinity were unharmed.

"Our little rivers, the San Fernando and the San Gabriel, approaching in broad sweep, unite six miles below, and are lost in the earth before reaching the ocean; it is probable that the beautiful plain, nearly circular and eight miles across, can be irrigated; then, flourishing like a garden, and overlooked by the snowy mouňtain, it might rival in beauty, as it must resemble, that of Grenada. It is a happiness to breathe the air, which gently stirs the vineyards and orange groves."

An express was sent to Monterey with a report of the attitude of the immigrant "battalion."

March 27th, the troops were moved to a carefully selected spot commanding the town.

"This place, whether the 'Paris of California' or not, is a hot bed of sedition, and originates all the rebellions or revolutions; and women, they say, play an influential part. It has come to my knowledge that the common talk is of the affair of the refused cannon; and that there soon will be more 'fun'; but they add that the Californians will join the men at San Miguel. That *sounds* badly."

Captain Smith returned the 28th; he had gone above sixty miles; he only discovered four Indians, who had murdered one, and wounded another man, and had stolen their animals; they were afoot, and ran to the near hills; the dragoons pursued and surrounded them, dismounted. The Indians, lying on their backs, defended themselves with arrows, which they shot with wonderful rapidity, wounding two of the men and several horses; they would not surrender and were all killed; they were naked, or had rabbit skins slung at their backs, as their sole covering. Some twenty horses were recovered.

"The dragoon horses came back with feet so worn as to make the most of them lame and useless. I shall to-morrow commence the introduction of horse-shoes in California, at least in this southern part. It would not suit the views of the Treasury Department to furnish two or three horses per man, California fashion; and it might not be of military convenience.' (The attempt failed for want of proper iron.)

Some Californians, this day rode out of town, at full speed, under fire of a few dragoons, a-foot, who had been ordered to arrest them; they had assaulted a countryman for having taken part with the Americans. It appears that an old regulation, closing drinking saloons on Sundays, has of late months been abrogated, and with very bad effects.

Lieutenant-colonel Fremont returned to Los Angeles March 30th.

Colonel R. B. Mason, first dragoons, had been sent to California in consequence of General Kearny's request to be relieved so soon as peace and order should follow on the conquest of California. He was now sent to Los Angeles, as an officer senior in army rank to Lieutenant-colonel Fremont, to enforce the discharge of the "battalion," and obedience to other orders. The New York regiment of volunteers, Colonel Stevenson, had arrived at Monterey; and two companies had taken post at Santa Barbara, and one at San Diego.

During all this period there were depredations by wild Indians, and exaggerated reports, and applications for military aid and protection, to the commander at Los Angeles; Captain A. J. Smith was sent to Cajon Pass, March 31st, with forty dragoons, in consequence of repeated calls for protection from an invasion of Piute Indians on the settlements of that vicinity.

The authority of Colonel Mason proved sufficient, with some difficulty, for the discharge of Lieutenant-colonel Fremont's men; and ten pieces of cannon were brought from the mission to Los Angeles. Only twenty-five horses were delivered.

Indian murders and depredations seemed to increase; it was believed that a body of Utahs, from far beyond the Territory, had invaded it. Colonel Mason, exercising a civil authority, addressed to alcaldes requisition to furnish Lieut.-colonel Cooke with all the men and horses he should demand. An expedition dependent upon this aid was planned by the latter, but failed for want of coöperation; but a company of the Mormon battalion was sent, April 11th, to establish a post at the Cajon Pass.

"The view from the hill overlooking the town is fine; the white-walled village is fully revealed, as at your feet; the meadows of the bright stream, intersected by many 'live fence' enclosures of vineyards, gardens and orchards; the Mesa extending above twenty miles, and the ocean beyond; on two sides, smooth green hills swell into mountains, which have the rich blue tints of a pure atmosphere, and are capped with snow-fields."

Report was received that the people near Cajon Pass refused, at first, to sell cattle; and will not send them to the post.

It is known that Indians—all savages—are very sympathetic with any warlike commotions; these evidently stir within them, and encourage their natural passions, and their cherished habits. It is probable that they were now thus incited to very unusual activity of aggression. But here, as in New Mexico, the Mexican power habitually ignored any duty of protection against them; and certainly now, the people were entirely remiss in any coöperation for their own protection, even in the matter of their abundant horses; and more, a general backwardness or unwillingness to sell horses for government use. Thus perhaps their applications and reports should have been treated with indifference; and there were indications, as there was rumor, of bad influences, of subtle intrigue. It was perhaps a mistake in Lieutenant-colonel Cooke, to yield, as far as he did, to his instincts of military protection.

April 19*th*.—" The irrigating canals are a source of considerable trouble and vexation ; not only as to distribution into fair shares, but in the matter of drinking, when foul clothes have been washed above.

" The native, of the best class, on occasion of ceremony is picturesque as well as very fine in costume. As a horseman he wears ever a jacket, but an ornamental one ; the trousers are open on the outer seams nearly to the waist, with many buttons, chiefly for ornament; they show thus, very white fine and voluminous drawers. They wear also, silk sashes of bright colors (from China). Stamped leather leggings, wonderful spurs, and the sombrero complete the picture."

It was ascertained, April 20th, that two men, in advance of a party of eleven, had arrived in Los Angeles from Sonora, and had presented passports to the alcalde,—who made no report. The men were confined, and examined separately; one of them had a passport which had been sent to him by Lieutenant-colonel Fremont; he had been a captain in the late hostilities,—and the other had been engaged in them, and wounded; giving a good account of themselves, they were released. But immediately after, it was reported through town that General Bustamente was approaching California at the head of a military force,—and then more definitely, a force of fifteen hundred men.

An intelligent Spanish gentleman was communicated with; he gave positive information that the Mexican Government had appropriated $600,000 toward this expedition, and that artillery and other arms and stores, had been collected at Acapulco; and also that one Limentura, whose vessel had lately been seized at San Pedro, had brought commissions, of high rank, for Californians. This gentleman detailed extraordinary indications, in the southern district, of an expected resort to arms, and was of opinion that there would be an insurrection, whether external aid came or not, unless the American forces were increased in this quarter; that the natives no more regarded the troops at Monterey than if they were at Boston.

It was soon ascertained that Limentura had landed cannon, etc., at San Vincente or San Thomas

—twelve miles apart—and near the Lower California line. There was a general excitement, and threatening demonstrations, accompanying these reports, whether true or false.

All measures of precaution were immediately but very quietly taken; an officers' party of dragoons was sent to Warner's rancho, Agua Caliente, to patrol the Sonora road as far as the desert; the company at Cajon Pass was withdrawn, the park of artillery was brought from camp into town, to the dragoon quarters, and three pieces manned by dragoons. The construction of a fort on the hill, fully commanding the town, which had been previously determined upon, was begun, and a company of infantry there posted. An express was sent to the commanding-general at Monterey.

A communication was also sent to Commodore Stockton, still at San Diego, giving full and minute information of the landing of the stores; and informing him that the lower road, easiest for General Bustamente, if coming, fell into the coast road at San Vincente; it was suggested that it would be well to send the sloop *Julia*, very quietly, to capture the cannon and stores.

Meanwhile the patrol had observed a collection of horses, which were being driven for concealment into cañons; and a traveller from Santa Barbara encountered twenty armed men, with the Mexican flag displayed. A race was announced at Santa Anna, eight or ten miles from Los Angeles, for Sunday April 25, and without the license required by Mexican law and usage. It was not stopped; and it was attended by nearly all the males of Los Angeles (including some confidential observers). This meeting was kept up until late at night; and undoubtedly it was then decided to await the actual arrival of reinforcements from Mexico. Lieutenant-colonel Fremont, two weeks previously, had informed Colonel Mason that his business would be finished in two or three days, when, as ordered, he would set out for Monterey; but he still lingered at Los Angeles.

April 28th, an answer was received from Commodore Stockton; he promised to sail to find and seize the deposit of arms, as soon as he could get the *Congress* out of the harbor; he added, "if Bustamente comes this road, he will not go far without some broken shins and bloody noses." The *Julia* came to San Pedro, April 30th, Lieutenant Selden commander, bringing an application from Commodore Stockton for four-pounders, to be used against Bustamente; he had sailed in the *Congress*. As most of the ammunition at Los Angeles was for four-pounders, they were not sent.

A report was received, May 3d, through the best available sources of information, that General Bustamente had crossed the Gulf, near its head, in boats of the pearl fishers; and, at last information was at a rancho on the western coast, seventy leagues below San Diego. The same day a return courier from Monterey gave information that two companies of the New York volunteers would be sent to Los Angeles.

The arrival of large reinforcements from New York, and the preparations for his reception, are among the probable causes of the miscarriage of General Bustamente's expedition.

Meantime, while immigration had been largely increasing, San Francisco, whose existence counted by months, showed great vitality and growth; fifty houses had gone up in a month; its population was American; General Kearny, aided by the arrival of troops and large amounts of mechanical means, and stores of all sorts, was fast establishing confidence and order throughout. March 10th, following Mexican law and custom, he granted to the town of San Francisco,—to be sold at auction for its benefit, —the beach and water lots; thus providing for wharves and docks, for the accommodation of a commerce which was growing beyond all precedent; merchant vessels were arriving almost daily; already the editor of a newspaper there established, was predicting its destiny to be the " Liverpool or New York of the Pacific Ocean."

In March, also, General Kearny inaugurated the first beginning of a mail service in the Territory; a horse mail was established every two weeks each way, between San Francisco and San Diego.

General Kearny arrived at Los Angeles May 9th; he had come to San Pedro in the store-ship *Lexington;* and with him were Colonel Stevenson and two companies of the New York regiment. Lieutenant-colonel Fremont was then sent to Monterey to be thence ordered to Fort Leavenworth.

The General and Governor was at this time looking to his speedy return, overland, to the United

States; availing himself of the permission accorded to his application made at Santa Fè, to return " in the event of our getting possession of Upper California—of establishing a civil government there,—securing peace, quiet and order among the inhabitants, and precluding the possibility of the Mexicans again having control there."

The time of service of the Mormon battalion expired in July, and the acceptance of the resignation of its Lieutenant-colonel commanding having been earnestly urged by him, in order that he might also return by this opportunity, it was accepted by General Kearny, May 13th, and he embarked, next day, with him and his suit, on the *Lexington* at San Pedro for Monterey.

After a pleasant voyage, lengthened by calms, the *Lexington* sailed into the picturesque but not always safe bay and harbor of Monterey, May 27th. " A most beautiful view presented itself; in the foreground eight vessels of war and some merchantmen were riding at anchor; beyond, the green slopes of the town and its environs, enclosed by a perfect semi-circle of rounded hills, chequered and sprinkled with the dark pines. Nature with its graceful variety here outdid itself in a distribution of slope and grove, valley and hilltop, which formed a combination of the *unsought effect*, which taste and art could not equal on this scale of magnificence; a grandeur, which, stopping short of the sublime, is the perfection of the beautiful."

The *Columbus*, ninety guns, was then in the harbor, and Commodore Biddle was Naval Commander-in-chief.

Leaving Colonel R. B. Mason, First Dragoons, Military Commander and Governor, in his place, General Kearny, May 31st, with numerous officers, constituting, with attendants, about forty men, (exclusive of Lieutenant-colonel Fremont's large party), and divided into convenient small messes, set out upon what proved a hard ride; one which averaged thirty-three miles a day for eighty-three days, without one of rest. Their provisions were exhausted, while in a corner of the territory of the Oregon of that day; but they soon met, as expected, the head of the great column of migration, extending then perhaps, a thousand miles.

The sequel of the military conquest is told in few words; for the poor natives of that great country, and all their discontent and restlessness, their hatred, threats, and seditions, were soon to be overwhelmed and extinguished, as by the stroke of Fate. Two men, discharged from the Mormon battalion, and employed by Captain Sutter to dig a mill-race, a few months later discovered, in prodigal abundance, placer GOLD.

THE END.

www.ingramcontent.com/pod-product-compliance
Lightning Source LLC
Chambersburg PA
CBHW031902220426
43663CB00006B/738